HEY! GOD,
Was That You?

Coincidences from over Five Thousand
Hours of Flight and Forty-Four Years

RON GLUCK

WESTBOW°
PRESS
A DIVISION OF THOMAS NELSON
& ZONDERVAN

WestBow Press books may be ordered through booksellers or by contacting:

WestBow Press
A Division of Thomas Nelson
1663 Liberty Drive
Bloomington, IN 47403
www.westbowpress.com
1 (866) 928-1240

Because of the dynamic nature of the Internet, any web addresses or
links contained in this book may have changed since publication and
may no longer be valid. The views expressed in this work are solely those
of the author and do not necessarily reflect the views of the publisher,
and the publisher hereby disclaims any responsibility for them.

Any people depicted in stock imagery provided by Thinkstock are models,
and such images are being used for illustrative purposes only.
Certain stock imagery © Thinkstock.

ISBN: 978-1-4908-1867-2 (sc)
ISBN: 978-1-4908-1869-6 (hc)
ISBN: 978-1-4908-1868-9 (e)

Library of Congress Control Number: 2013922122

Printed in the United States of America.

WestBow Press rev. date: 01/13/2014

This book is dedicated to all those engaged in or supporting the unraveling of languages, reassembling them into written form, and assuring the translation of the Word of God so that people worldwide can have Scriptures in the language they think in—their mother tongue—and to Arthur and Hulda, Ruth, Cheryl, Trent and Kelly, Sharon, Charles and Jennifer, and Owen and John.

Good judgment comes from experience, and a lot of that comes from bad judgment.
—Will Rogers

CONTENTS

SIL International (formerly the Summer Institute of Linguistics), JAARS, and Wycliffe Bible Translators are partner nonprofit agencies. See Technical Stuff for websites.

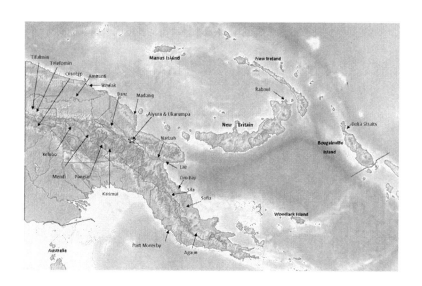

Map of the Trust Territory of Papua and New Guinea

March 1965—November 1969 based on UN Map 4104

INTRODUCTION

In 1959, I was aligned for takeoff shortly before noon at the Greater Pittsburgh Airport in a Pennsylvania Air National Guard F86L all-weather fighter interceptor jet. The air was warm, the wind was calm, and the sky was clear with high overcast—excellent for flying. In my helmet headphones, I heard Pit Tower clear a TWA Connie (Constellation) passenger plane onto runway ten and to "hold position." The Connie taxied into position on the opposite end of runway twenty-eight, my runway. With brakes locked, I advanced the throttle. While awaiting the engine spool-up to maximum revs, I lowered the flaps to takeoff position and checked the circuit breakers and flight controls before going up on a routine training flight. There was no way of knowing that what would happen in the next twelve to eighteen seconds would foreshadow coincidences in future years.

The engine was howling at max revs, eight thousand revolutions per minute. All instruments were in the green, so I radioed, "Pit Tower, Barney fifty-eight ready," and was cleared for takeoff. I advanced the throttle to the far forward détente, and the afterburner kicked in, adding maximum thrust. The tailpipe temp gauge stayed in the green, so I released the brakes. The eighty-six began rolling, slowly at first with full fuel tanks and then accelerating more quickly down the 7,500-foot runway.

Approaching the five-thousand-foot mark, the plane became airborne and climbed ten to twenty feet with indicated airspeed passing through 125 knots (nautical miles per hour). I was about to reach forward to retract the wheels and flaps when engine noise and forward thrust stopped abruptly! The plane bounced hard back onto the runway and along with ten tons of metal and fuel, I hurtled down runway twenty-eight straight toward the four spinning propellers of the TWA Connie. That pilot screamed into the radio asking if I had him in sight. I was a little busy yanking the throttle back, deploying the drag chute, and trying to control the eighty-six, but blurted out, "Got ya eye-balled."

The drag chute slowed the plane rapidly, and as engine rpms spooled down, the hydraulic pressure also dropped, eliminating nose wheel steering. Trying to avoid the Connie, I stomped hard on the right pedal, hoping for sufficient rudder-air effect to steer off of the runway and into the grass. The eighty-six rolled slower and slower, finally onto the grass, my left wingtip passing just feet under the TWA left wingtip, and slowly onto a concrete taxiway, where I braked to a stop. Securing the cockpit, I opened the canopy and turned off the master power switch. At some point I had shouted into the radio for a crash crew. They promptly pulled up in emergency vehicles and helped me exit the plane.

Back at the Guard flight operations, I was asked why takeoff was aborted. My explanation was that the engine flamed out.

The squadron commander then assigned me to fly a different eighty-six. In trying to get up into the cockpit of the second plane, my legs wouldn't work. That is, I could not get myself up the ladder and into the cockpit. The squadron commander was watching, saw that I was in distress, and ordered me to go home and fly another day.

The events of that day over fifty years ago still come to mind.

In retrospect, how grateful I am to the Pennsylvania Air National Guard 147th fighter interceptor squadron for the hours of mandatory training in the flight simulator—an exact replica of that model eighty-six cockpit. Many sessions were practice for just such emergencies. At a critical instant, when seconds literally counted, there was no hesitation pulling out that lever to deploy the drag chute. It was an automatic reaction.

But consider a few what-if questions.

1. If the eighty-six engine had flamed out just *one* second later, I would have been higher, touched down several hundred feet closer to or right on top of the Connie, and . . .?
2. That eighty-six was later towed to the Guard "cabbage patch" test area. The engine was started, the afterburner kicked in, and the engine flamed out

again, but the throttle was left untouched. Suddenly the engine exploded. Thankfully, no one was hurt. But why didn't it explode during my aborted takeoff?

3. Was our Maker involved in protecting those aboard the TWA plane—and me—that day?

"LORD, I DIDN'T COME HERE TO FLY DEAD PIGS!"

One morning in 1967, the other SIL pilots and I were at the hangar refueling and pre-flighting (inspecting) our planes for the day's flying. The daily radio check-in was occurring with SIL language teams requesting flights as John Sahlin, the new flight coordinator and voice of Uniform Whiskey* gave the day's flight schedule. In the background of all the radio chatter, I was hearing a distinct, intermittent clicking sound. *Could it be someone trying to transmit but unable to?* I asked John to listen for it. He heard it too and asked everyone else on the net to be quiet and just listen. Sure enough, there was that clicking sound.

John radioed, "This is Uniform Whiskey. If anyone is having problems transmitting, click the mic button twice."

We heard two clicks of a mic button. Then John called the village teams he had not yet spoken with, soon determining that Dottie and Edie, the West sisters, had the radio problem.

John next instructed them, "Use one click for no and two clicks for yes to answer my questions."

"Is your radio okay?"

Two clicks.

"Is the radio battery low?"

Two clicks.

"Can you hear okay?"

Two clicks.

"Okay, we'll change the flight schedule and get a charged battery out to you this morning."

I took the flight—eleven minute trip direct to their airstrip, Imani, about twenty miles southeast of Ukarumpa, our SIL center. The flight would take me over the steep-sided Imani Valley, whose eponymous landing strip was one-way and sloped, maybe 3,400 feet above sea level. One could only land uphill, into the closed canyon. Once committed on final approach, there was no second chance. I began a circling descent, lined up for final approach into the narrow valley, and landed. As I got out of the plane, it was hot, and as usual there were plenty of flies. People gathered around as I unloaded the charged twelve-volt car battery for the two-way radio and other cargo to resupply the village store. Those batteries weighed nearly forty pounds.

Dottie and Edie were grateful and glad to see me. "By the way," they told me, "there are five men here who would like to be flown to Leron Plains. They can pay. Can you take them?"

"Sure. Have them stand alone with their baggage."

Since landing, I had detected a strong, pungent, putrid odor, but couldn't discern its source. The five village men I was to fly stood together with their personal effects in expandable woven bark bags slung over their shoulders. From under the pilot seat, I removed a small bathroom scale, put it on the ground, and weighed each of them on it. I scaled their bags separately and loaded the bags into the belly cargo pod under the 185, a Cessna single engine plane. The heaviest of the men may have weighed one hundred pounds. I weighed the fifth man, and his bag was the heaviest. Through his woven bag, I could see inside what appeared to be an animal carcass. A second glance showed it to be a pig, sliced neatly in half, foaming and covered with crawling maggots—the source of the odor, some twenty-five pounds of it. My stomach turned; I jumped to my feet and ran a ways down the airstrip to breathe some fresh air, at the same time starting a one-way conversation with God.

Lord, I didn't come here to fly dead pigs! I could be piloting a nice, air-conditioned jetliner, making decent money . . .

After a few moments of breathing clean air, I calmed down, and the Lord got my attention. What immediately became apparent was an attitude problem—selfishness on my part. He had led me to New Guinea to serve these people, and yes, it did include flying the men's meat supply to take on their journey.

Realizing I'd been wrong I asked for his forgiveness and began walking back toward the airplane. Filling my lungs with a big gulp of fresh air I held my breath and ran the rest of the way, quickly putting the bag of smelly pig carcass into the pod, secured the pod door, and then resumed breathing. I motioned for the men to get in the plane, helping them secure their shoulder and seat belts, waved good-bye to Dottie and Edie, and then flew the men to Leron Plains, an isolated dirt airstrip in the middle of the Markham Valley. After taking off from Imani, I never turned the plane. It was a short, straight, six-minute hop that likely saved the men, at minimum, a day's hike.

On landing, they got out of the plane and looked around, smiling and talked excitedly. There were no buildings, and the place was deserted. I opened the pod and removed their baggage—including their meat supply. Slinging the bags over their shoulders, the five men shook my hand and walked away, talking animatedly. As I took off, from the corner of my eye I saw them still talking, laughing, and gesturing as they walked—satisfied passengers, I assumed.

*Each ground transceiver was licensed by the Australian Government and assigned two letters for identification. The hangar radio was UW and the International Phonetic Alphabet was used for communication. U is Uniform and W is Whiskey; hence, "Uniform Whiskey".

DIFFERENT FROM YESTERDAY

It was a little unusual to fly to an out-of-the-way airstrip two days in succession, but it happened in 1966. Harland Kerr, an SIL linguist at Pangia, told me upon landing on the second day that one of the Wiru men—of the ethnic group the Kerrs lived with—said the airplane was different that day from the one I had come in the previous day. I answered, "But Harland, it's the same plane. Ask him what's different."

In his Wiru tongue, the man responded, "Yesterday, the plane had a rounded propeller tip, but today, the propeller is square-tipped."

I nodded my head, admitting, "Harland, he's right! We changed the prop!"

Who had given those observation skills to this Wiru man?

3

STAY AWAY—IT'S RAINING CATS AND DOGS HERE!

A New Tribes missionary stationed at Wonenara had booked a flight well in advance. He and his wife were much in need of a break and were looking forward to time by the ocean at the coastal town of Lae. Located in a mountainous area, the Wonenara airstrip was a little tricky. From the side, it had the profile of a child's playground slide. Planes would land on the lower end and then add power to roll up to a level parking area dug out of the hillside on the left, three-fourths of the way up the "slide." Getting to the lower end to land was a little tricky.

I was not yet familiar with the weather systems that blew in from the south. Cloud coverage was low and thick. Time en route took almost double the usual seventeen minutes. Drizzle and low clouds obscured the ridges, making it necessary to fly under the cloud base and take a long route before finding the right valley. I turned east into the Wonenara Valley, passing the airstrip near the end of the valley. Making a 180 to the right onto a final approach, after clearing a small hill, I throttled back and lowered the flaps to decrease airspeed, drop down quickly, and touch down on the lower end. Then I added power to roll uphill to the parking area. On leaving, I would retrace this path and depart through the same valley—if the weather did not deteriorate.

With the plane parked, I could tell that taking off might be a challenge, because the wheels had thrown up gobs of mud now stuck to the underside of the wings. Before landing, I had made a mental note, deciding that if I couldn't see that small hill we needed to clear beyond the end of the runway, I would abort the flight and spend the night there.

I greeted the missionary, met his family, and weighed and loaded their baggage into the cargo pod. The hill we needed to clear on takeoff was still visible, so I motioned to the family to get into the plane. I checked the security of all their seat belts and shoulder harnesses and then climbed in and fastened my own. After starting the engine, I checked the magnetos, taxied onto the runway, and turned left, going uphill to the top for takeoff.

On the right side of the runway was a steep drop into the valley that we needed to fly out of. At the top of the airstrip, as I tried to turn the airplane 180 degrees around to the right, the plane began sliding sideways down the airstrip and toward that steep drop. Fuel began running out of the lower wing ram air vent. *Are we going to tip over?*

I pressed hard on the right-foot rudder pedal, adding full power to blow the tail around, thinking, *This really isn't good.*

I should park and spend the night here. Waiting for clearer, drier weather would be smart.

The plane was aligned for a downhill takeoff. I pressed the top of the rudder pedals to lock the wheel brakes, attempting to stop our slide downhill, because the hill we needed to clear was no longer visible. But even with wheels locked, the plane continued sliding down the runway. I was unable to stop the plane and risked sliding off over the sharp drop on the left. So I released the brakes and applied full throttle. Going downhill, we were soon airborne, carrying more mud into the drizzling rain and low cloud cover that now was almost fog.

The hill we needed to climb over in order to have adequate space to turn 180 degrees to exit the valley gradually emerged into view. The greatest struggle was not to pull back on the elevator control to climb faster—a sure recipe for disaster! We cleared that hill; I then lowered the nose to gain airspeed while retracting the flaps and turned a 180 to the left to exit the valley.

The missionary's wife, seated behind me, had been vocal in her fear throughout the takeoff until I lowered the nose and turned to exit the valley. As soon as we were airborne, I radioed Lae control with our departure time and indicated Aiyura (SIL's home airstrip) as my destination. (That info would give rescuers an idea of the route to search along in case we never made it to our destination—my first time ever thinking in such terms.)

Once out of the Wonenara Valley, I took a general north heading, expecting to land back home at Aiyura. Flying underneath the cloud base, I radioed Uniform Whiskey, SIL's flight coordinator, Ken Davis, at the hangar to advise him of our ETA in sixteen minutes.

His response: "Don't come here! It's raining cats and dogs." Soon we were in rain so hard I could not see anything except cloud through the windshield. But looking out the side window under the wing, I could see we had adequate altitude and clearance over nearby terrain.

Both fuel gauges were bouncing on empty. As long as they were bouncing, I knew we were okay, so we continued on a northeast heading, in and out of rain, out of the highlands and finally into the wide Markham Valley. But surprise! The Markham was full of clouds too. Thankfully, those clouds, at least, weren't hiding tall hills. Once assured the highlands were behind us, I headed east for the major town and coastal port of Lae, the original destination of my passengers, landing there without further incident. In all, a normally fifty-minute flight segment had taken nearly two hours. The children had fallen asleep en route, but their mom and dad and I were glad to be on terra firma.

After unloading their baggage, I climbed onto the wing strut and removed the fuel caps on top of each wing to check the remaining fuel. The dipstick showed none in either tank. Following valleys instead of flying the more direct path of crossing ridges, flying north instead of straight east into the Markham Valley, and changing altitudes several times had taken not only extra time but also considerably more fuel. The hazards of flying in poor weather and the associated dangers of operating in and out of slippery, muddy, sloped airstrips were not lost on me. Divine protection seemed obvious that day, overruling my poor judgment. Mud that the wheels had flung to the wing undersides at Wonenara had washed away.

Over time, I've thought frequently about this flight, and now, years later, I understand more of what happened that day. VH-SIM was a tail-wheel plane. When making a 180 at the top of the Wonenara airstrip to take off, I had turned the plane against P-factor (see Technical Stuff), the asymmetrical pull of the propeller. Mistakenly, I had turned right instead of left! If I had turned left, asymmetrical prop loading—that is, the right side of the propeller—would have helped in turning the plane left. I didn't think of it until now, forty-five years later, as I wrote and remembered the details of this flight.

In retrospect, waiting for better weather before flying that day would have been wiser. Shortly after this trip, ELTs (emergency locator transmitters) that Chief Pilot Jim Baptista had ordered were installed, one in each plane. In case of accident, a hard impact would actuate it to transmit a continuous screech for up to forty-eight hours so that search planes could home in to the accident site.

Recently I learned from Chuck Daly at JAARS that before Wonenara was closed permanently, SIL pilots followed a procedure. When turning a 180 at the top of the airstrip for takeoff, a left turn was mandatory in order to utilize engine torque and asymmetrical prop loading to facilitate the turn. In addition, the bulk of the fuel onboard was to be in the high or right wing tank to minimize loss of fuel through the left wing ram air fuel vent.

Was I unwise in making this flight? Obviously. It was poor judgment that thankfully became what Will Rogers termed *experience*.

4

THE PROPELLER WIND-MILLED

I will never forget one 185 flight in 1965 on a clear, sunny day. My experience flying in light aircraft was minimal at the time, maybe 500 hours, and I had not yet realized how critical it was to maintain or exceed airspeeds recommended by airplane manufacturers for sustained climbing.

By carrying minimum reserve fuel, I was able to take an eleven-hundred-pound payload from Lae to Kabwum, the village location of SILers Ken and Noreen McElhanon. In a fully loaded 185 at gross weight, Kabwum was a thirty-minute flight north of Lae, separated by an eleven-thousand-foot ridge of the Finisterre Mountains. Normal climb speed is ninety knots for the 185, but feeling rushed, I pulled back on the control wheel to raise the nose of the plane slightly to climb faster, though at a slower speed (eighty knots) while closely monitoring the engine cylinder head temperature gauge to be sure the cylinder head temp did not get excessive.

At 11,050 feet, parallel to the ridge and about fifty feet above it, I leveled the plane to regain some airspeed. Then, when I was about to cross over to the Kabwum side, the engine quit without warning! Instinctively, I lowered the nose to maintain airspeed and headed away from the ridge back toward Lae on the seacoast. Gliding airspeed was sufficient to cause the prop to continue turning or wind-milling. The engine silence was penetrated by outside air whistling through the air vents. There were no flat places on the ridge to land. While in gliding descent away from the ridge, I glanced at the engine instruments and fuel tank gauges. There was adequate fuel, and all the gauges were in the green. Indicated airspeed was one-hundred–plus knots, so I flipped the auxiliary fuel pump switch on. The engine and wind-milling prop immediately came to life. Insufficient airspeed, I assumed, had caused the air-cooled engine to overheat.

In gliding, the plane had lost altitude, descending to 9,500 feet, where I maintained level flight for one or two minutes at one hundred knots. The cylinder head temp had cooled a tad, and engine operation seemed normal, so I switched off the fuel pump. The engine continued smoothly, not missing a beat. I decided to try crossing the ridge again, pulling back the control wheel to regain the 1,550 feet of altitude lost, this time climbing fifteen knots faster, at ninety-five knots, to ram more cooling air into the engine compartment. All seemed well, so I crossed over the ridge with 150 feet of additional clearance, reduced power to descend, and landed at Kabwum. After greeting Ken and handing him his mail and fresh meat, I unloaded the cargo, got back into the plane, and returned to Lae without further incident.

For the rest of that day, the issue of following recommended airspeeds, procedures, and operations by aircraft manufacturers was seared right into the eyelids of my memory.

Chief Pilot Jim Baptista confirmed that inadequate cooling could also cause heated 100/130-octane avgas to vapor lock, or turn from liquid to a gaseous mix, at higher altitudes because of less dense atmospheric pressure. For no-frills 185 airplanes (meaning no turbocharger to boost engine performance in order to attain higher altitude), carrying a maximum load to 11,050 feet was, therefore, definitely "at altitude"!

But who or what kept me from attempting to cross the ridge just before the engine quit?

Trivia: At an altitude of fourteen thousand feet, the earth's atmospheric pressure is one-half of the atmospheric pressure at sea level.

5

POINTERS! WHAT ARE THEY DOING?

In 1965, on one of my first solo trips to Lae, I reported VH-SIM's position at Nadzap, the 5,800-foot-long asphalt World War II runway, ten minutes west of Lae. An Australian controller, Jeff, radioed back, "Roger, Sierra India Mike. Exercise caution on landing. There are pointers at the northwest end of the runway."

I requested the controller to repeat his transmission, which he did. I then asked my lone, Australian passenger* if he heard the tower.

"Sure, I heard him. He said there are pointers and to report at the Markham Bridge."

Now three minutes out, I reported at the Markham Bridge, and the controller cleared me to continue approach and again to exercise caution on final approach because of the pointers at the end of the runway. A few minutes later, he cleared me to land, making mention of the pointers for the third time, and I had to ask, "What are the pointers doing?"

"They are pointing," the controller answered.

"Right," I answered, descending lower and slower on final approach. Looking ahead, I observed men on the end of the runway, *painting* white lines!

My understanding of "Strine"—Australian English—was in its infancy.

*This passenger was a rancher. SIL aircraft frequently carried non-SIL personnel on a space-available basis. On occasion other agencies, including government, chartered the SIL planes.

6

WHAT'S BITCHUMEN?

When flying out of airports with control towers, submitting a written flight plan to the tower controllers was a requirement. As a result, I got to know them personally. On one of my early flights to Lae, after landing, Jeff, the controller, directed me to turn off of the runway onto the first "bitchumen" taxiway. I had no idea what he meant. After he used the term several times, I asked on the radio, "What's *bitchumen*?"

Jeff's colleague, John, another Australian, answered my query, "He means bituminous, Ron."

After refueling and securing my next cargo load, I walked to the Lae tower to file a flight plan, asking John about the *bitchumen* term. He explained that what we call blacktop or asphalt in the United States, Aussies call *bitchumen* or *bituminous*. That was Strine. I soon learned that although Australians and Americans share a common language, a few words are spoken or used differently—a flashlight was a torch, dinner was tea, etc.

My learning of Strine was slow and woefully deficient. The problems of slight dialectical difference in the same language only emphasized the difficulties that learners of English experience.

7

PIGS AND KIDS—DIFFERENT VALUES

The Lutheran Mission chartered an SIL plane to transport one of its national church pastors and his family. I flew to Wantoat, where they were waiting. The airstrip is located on top of a mesa—a flat-topped hill, barely long enough to land and take off, with abrupt drop-offs on both ends. The pastor had four children plus baggage and a live pig. I weighed everything: the people, the baggage, and the pig. Wantoat was close to five thousand feet elevation, and we were fifty pounds overweight for takeoff, which also was the weight of the pig. I told the pastor we had to leave something behind, assuming, of course, it would be the pig. Instead, he instructed his eleven-year old son to walk across the eleven-thousand-foot Finisterre Mountains to Saidor, a trek that would require at least more than a day. But the pastor and rest of the family and pig were there in less than twenty-five minutes.

My initial understanding then was simply this: different cultures, different values.

Over time, however, I realized that pigs were equivalent to one's bank account. The pastor's decision for the pig to fly did not reflect adversely on his love for his son.

8

STRENGTH OF STEEL

My first scheduled flight of the day was an hour-and-twenty-minute hop to Nipa in the Western Highlands, carrying cargo to Vic Schlatter of the Apostolic Christian Mission. I had been flying in PNG for more than two years now.

In loading the 185 with long, cumbersome cargo, flight coordinator Ken Davis had taken off the right door and removed the right front and middle seats in order to load lengths of corrugated steel sheeting. The sheeting alone weighed 850 pounds. We secured it to the floor so it would not shift position during flight. It occupied space normally taken by the right front, middle, and rear seats, extending into the cabin from the rear bulkhead to the right front doorpost, almost up to the ceiling. Only the pilot seat remained in the plane.

The right door was remounted and locked. From the left front seat there was enough room for me to see the instrument panel and reach the cowl flap and wing flap levers. With some effort I could raise myself high enough to see over the sheeting and out the starboard (right) side. I had made cargo flights like this before. This Nipa trip would be a piece of cake!

After a routine preflight and engine startup, I taxied to the end of the runway, did engine and control checks, checked instruments, aligned the gyrocompass to the runway heading, and then took off, climbing to an altitude of 8,500 feet on a westerly course that would take me straight to Nipa. In the process I radioed DCA and Vic in that order with an ETA. My course would be parallel to but track south of the Wahgi Valley and included thirty minutes over a green carpet of forest—void, I believed, of human life.

Although the weather had been clear at takeoff, cloud coverage increased along the way. I glanced increasingly often at the gyrocompass while flying around clouds to resume a westerly heading.

Although the gyrocompass was set before takeoff, lots of maneuvering of the plane and changes of direction in-flight sometimes necessitates realignment of the gyro to the magnetic compass, which was mounted in the center of the 185 windshield.

A quick glance at the mag compass got my attention. Then I stared at it, unable to believe what I was seeing. The compass floats in liquid and though it normally bounces around in flight, it provides reliable general compass headings. But this one was not bouncing. It was fixed in place, not moving when I made turns. I made a quick forty-five-degree turn and then turned back to what I thought was on course, and it never budged, although the liquid in it was sloshing around.

Ahh yes, the sheets of corrugated steel on board—850 pounds of it. I'd forgotten! Steel is a ferrous metal. When in close proximity to a magnet, steel alters electromagnetic fields, including that of a simple magnetic compass.

I did find Nipa and landed a few minutes late. After exchanging greetings, Vic and I removed the right front door and the corrugated sheeting. As the last sheet was taken from the plane, the mag compass swung freely back to its normal level position atop the liquid, with the slightest hint of appearing saucy—or, as the Aussies would say, cheeky. To me, and no one else, the mag compass seemed to say, "It serves ya right for not really giving me the time of day before taking off, mate!"

My routine preflight check of the instruments before takeoff had completely missed the skewed mag compass on the windshield. One result of this omission was the installation of new flip-tab checklists with ten flip-tabs on top of the instrument panel of each plane. Each time the item was checked before takeoff, that particular tab was flipped up. Before landing, as items were checked, the tabs were flipped down.

In retrospect, fifty years later, I now wonder—what other unnoticed forces have impacted the directions chosen in life?

9

I COULDN'T BELIEVE IT!

The Methodist Mission had chartered an SIL plane to shuttle cargo from Nipa to the town of Mendi. As the proverbial crow flies, the distance was not far, perhaps twenty miles. Both airstrips were at an elevation of roughly five thousand feet but separated by an eight-thousand-foot mountain ridge.

Jim Baptista had set an SIL takeoff payload weight limit of six hundred pounds out of Nipa in a 185. The first two shuttle flights to Mendi and back were uneventful. On the third and final one, I agreed to take an extra fifty pounds of cargo. It was past noon, the rainy season had started, and the wind would soon begin to pick up. Unaware that during the second shuttle, a light rain shower had come and gone, leaving a few puddles on the far end of the Nipa airstrip, I taxied to the end of the strip with the 650-pound load, checked engine magnetos, and waited. When the wind sock on the far end of the runway showed a solid headwind, I advanced the throttle forward to take off.

At just beyond halfway down the runway, the plane slowed as one wheel went through a puddle. Monitoring airspeed closely,

I could hardly believe what I was seeing. Beyond the halfway point on the runway, the airspeed indicator was showing that airspeed had decreased from fifty to just less than forty knots. I glanced at the windsock at the far end; it was blowing straight out, but in the opposite direction. A strong tailwind was now blowing, causing a faster ground speed but slower airspeed. The throttle was full forward, and the plane was still on the ground with an indicated airspeed of barely forty knots.

Less than a few hundred feet of runway remained. I had fast ground speed and low airspeed, and not enough runway remained to abort the take off—in sum, a terrible combination!

"God save me!" I shouted. Simultaneously, the airspeed indicator jumped to above fifty knots, and, just as quickly, the plane was airborne, barely missing trees beyond the runway. Airspeed continued increasing rapidly as the wings rose higher above treetop level and a normal climb-out speed then easily carried the 185 over the eight-thousand-foot mountain ridge to Mendi.

In retrospect, the extra fifty pounds on board had little effect in extending the takeoff roll. Instead, it was water puddles and the 180-degree change in wind direction from a solid headwind to a strong tailwind, pushing from behind and extending the takeoff roll that I hadn't picked up on.

God had intervened—again. And a new guideline was made to nix afternoon takeoffs out of Nipa during rainy season.

10

SURASIL AND SIGN LANGUAGE

The Department of Civil Aviation at Lae contacted SIL, asking if we could make a medical emergency flight out of Surasil, a small airstrip toward the western end of the Markham Valley. I made the twelve-minute flight from Aiyura. Upon landing, a young woman, obviously pregnant, was waiting. She looked to be about twelve years old and was scared. I tried to be gentle, helping her into the plane, securing her seat belt, and flew her to Lae. In transmitting my estimated arrival time to Lae Tower, I also requested that an ambulance meet the plane. And sure enough, an ambulance was waiting, and the driver took the woman to Lae Hospital.

A week later, another flight was scheduled to transport the woman and her newborn back to Surasil. In English I asked, "Is it a baby boy or baby girl?" She didn't understand. So in pidgin I asked, *"Em i pikinini man ou pikinini meri?"* Again she looked puzzled. Suddenly, her face brightened, and smiling, she took her infant by the feet and held it naked upside down so I could see it was a girl. A very pleased young mother exited the plane back at Surasil with her infant twenty-two minutes later, still smiling.

11

YOU MISSED THE SHEET!

Late one afternoon, flying was done for the day and Jim Entz (SIL's Chief of Aviation Maintenance) and I were still at the hangar getting ready to lock up. The hangar radio, Uniform Whiskey was still turned on and amid heavy static normal for that time of day we suddenly heard a woman's voice calling, "Uniform Whiskey, Uniform Whiskey" asking for help. It was one of the Margarets from the Margaret Wells/Margaret Matheison SIL language team in the village.

After repeated attempts, we got the message straight amid the static: a young child had respiratory problems and needed oxygen. Was there any way we could get oxygen to their village that afternoon? It was then close to 4:30 p.m. The sky was cloudy, and rain threatened. An hour of daylight remained.

Jim quickly got a lightweight bottle of oxygen with a face mask from hanger supplies, while I checked for adequate fuel in a 185—we always carried an extra hour of reserve fuel.

Our plan: find their location, fly over it, drop the oxygen, and return. The Margarets were in a village on the coast, just on the north side of the Finisterre Mountain Range, studying the Siroi Language. It would take about twenty minutes in good weather, but towering clouds would cover those mountains. If weather on the north side of the Finnisterres deteriorated, preventing us from returning home, we could always head north, follow the coast a few miles, and land at Madang, a large port town on the coast, to spend the night.

Jim and I took off and headed toward Shaggy Ridge Gap, on the north side of the Ramu Valley, a low-level 4,100-foot pass crossing the Finnisterre range, found it open, and flew through just under the cloud base at 4,500 feet, and then headed for the coast. I didn't know the exact coastal location of the Margarets, but soon they heard the plane and directed us on the radio toward their house near the beach. I retarded the throttle to descend while heading toward them.

"You're going to fly right over us!" one of them yelled. The sound of the plane roared via their microphone through our plane radio speakers. I made two low passes a few feet above the trees, but neither Jim nor I could see their house with a grass thatch roof under palm trees. It blended in with everything else.

I suggested they spread a bed sheet on the beach next to the ocean for a target, did a wide turn to allow them time to get a sheet stretched out on the beach, and then lowered the flaps, slowing the plane to forty-five knots for a third pass at treetop level. We saw the sheet; Jim had opened the plane door window on his side and was holding the bottle with attached face mask outside the door. When I yelled, "Drop!" he released his grip of them.

They quickly radioed, saying, "You missed the sheet!"

"By how much?"

"Two feet!"

"Neither of us were bombardiers," I explained.

They thanked us; we were able to return through Shaggy Ridge Gap, landing back home under a darker sky but thankful the airdrop had been achieved in spite of threatening, weather. After the mile motorcycle ride from the hangar back to our homes at Ukarumpa, it rained hard.

A radio message the next morning said the oxygen had helped. The child survived.

Question: who is the source of good ideas, anyway—a white bed sheet stretched out on the beach?

12

KASSAM PASS OUT

In March 1967, the Kassam Pass, an important section of road linking PNG's highlands to the seaport of Lae, washed out from heavy rains. It was then the only road by which heavy supply shipments were received at Ukarumpa, where several hundred SIL personnel and their families lived. When told it would take several weeks for the road to be repaired, another plan evolved.

An 18-wheeler trailer truck, packed with supplies for SIL was driven from Lae to Gusap, a 5,200-foot long World War II airstrip on the floor of the Markham Valley and nearest to the bottom of the Kassam Pass. The plan was for Willis Baughman and me, the only pilots available, each to shuttle supplies in a 185 "uphill" from Gusap to Aiyura until the truck was empty. As the crow flies, it was a distance of only sixteen to seventeen miles. With maximum allowable loads in the 185s, it was taking just eleven minutes to make the four-thousand-feet altitude climb to Aiyura. The return empty flight "downhill" was only eight minutes. Unloading the truck, loading the planes, and securing the loads inside each plane was taking twenty to thirty minutes, even with the aid of two New Guinea employees—one helping to unload the truck, and the other helping to load the planes.

At Aiyura, the process was reversed; unloading the planes went faster, but an hour for a round trip shuttle seemed average. It was hot work, but I felt challenged to lower my round-trip times by loading and unloading faster.

My logbook indicates I flew ten shuttles totaling 3:25 flight hours that day; I assume Willis's logbook had a similar entry. By 4:00 p.m. that afternoon the trailer had been emptied, and the truck driver began his return trip to Lae. Those supplies at Ukarumpa lasted until after the Kassam Pass had been repaired and reopened. I frequently think of that day—but primarily for another reason.

Willis was about ten years older than me. We were taking turns. After his 185 was loaded and the cargo secured, he would fly to Aiyura, unload, and make the return trip. As soon as his plane was loaded and he was taxiing to takeoff for Aiyura, I would start loading the second 185 and do the same drill. It was taking him a bit longer than me to complete a round-trip shuttle. At midday, I caught up with him at Gusap, our 185s both empty and ready for loading. Willis, being the senior pilot, told me that since it was taking me less time to complete a shuttle, I should go ahead of him and load my plane first, which I gladly did.

In retrospect, I now wish I had refused and instead helped him load his plane. My competitive spirit was way out of line. It was a habit carried over from my air force days and sorely in need of a reality check—I just didn't know it, yet.

13

RED DIRT!

It is interesting that in the seventy-ninth year of my life, a 185 flight in PNG of more than forty years ago came to mind—again. The last bit of a five-hour flight was the two-and-one-half-hour return leg from Sofia in the Popendetta region, 250 miles southeast of Lae. It was late afternoon, and Harry Weimer, newly elected SIL director in PNG, was my lone passenger. Cloud coverage was virtually eight-eighths, meaning almost complete coverage, but it wasn't high. Climbing up through an occasional hole, I was able finally to get on top of the clouds, and for the next 120 minutes we maintained an altitude of 8,500 feet in clear, smooth air, holding a northwest compass heading, touching occasional cloud tops. There was no visible ground reference to confirm our actual position, but I could tell generally where we were because the clouds closely hugged the terrain. I knew we were entering the Markham Valley but wasn't sure what part. Harry, seated next to me, had fallen asleep. Given that we had spent more than two hours above the clouds, I was growing concerned as to our exact position, wondering if winds had blown us off course or slowed our ground speed.

For some reason, I turned my head left, just in time to see a hole in the clouds a mile off the left wingtip. Banking abruptly in that direction awakened Harry, but I needed to get to the hole, which was about to close. Looking down through it, I spotted a north-south airstrip of red dirt. *Red dirt!* There was only one red dirt north-south airstrip then that was south of the Markham Valley: Langimar, where I had spent a day helping Hap Skinner with its recent construction. (He had come up with a unique way of moving dirt by redirecting the natural course of spring water flowing from the higher end of the sloped strip.) The quartering headwind had blown us well south off course, by maybe four miles, also slowing our ground speed. I made a course correction, and within twenty-five minutes we were descending on a downwind leg and landing at Aiyura.

Questions:

1. What caused me to turn my head *left* at just that instant, instead of right, before the cloud hole vanished?
2. If I had not spent that day at Langimar a few months earlier helping Hap Skinner, would I have recognized our exact position?
3. Does He who created clouds not still control them?

14

SO FINELY TUNED

In 1966 after several weeks of heavy flying, I became ill and was confined to bed for two days. Upon resuming flight duties, I noticed something different while departing from Lae in the twin-engine Aztec. The plane was loaded to a maximum allowable takeoff weight of 5,200 pounds, and as soon as it became airborne, I could tell right away that my hand and finger coordination on the controls had lost a very, very fine control touch—and after only two days' absence. I never realized one's touch on the controls could be so finely attuned.

I'd forgotten the gentle touch necessary a few years earlier when flying at fast speeds in formation, staying just a few feet tucked under the wing of the flight leader's plane.

Could the same be true of one's spiritual walk, I wonder—losing touch if regular times of communing with one's Maker are neglected?

15

NO ONE SHOULD HAVE
TO EAT WORMS

In 1965 Leon and Betty Schanely had begun studying a language spoken by a group in the Sepik River area. On their first trip to the village, they had taken only enough supplies and food to last thirty days, because they figured that by then they would know enough of the language to buy food from the local people. But alas, the thirtieth day was approaching, and they were nowhere near attaining the language-learning goals they had set. On day twenty-nine, they opened their last can of food, spaghetti, and prayed a long prayer over it, seeking God's blessing.

While eating their spaghetti dinner, they sadly concluded they would need to radio a request for a plane to come and pick them up the next morning.

But very early the following day, there was a cough outside their window (the cultural way to announce one's presence in PNG). It was the village chief, who said to them in broken Pidgin

English, "I saw what you ate last night and am truly sorry. I will have our women bring you good food so that you won't get sick. No one should have to eat *worms*."

Question: where did the chief's concern for Schanelys originate?

16

YOU WERE SCARED, WEREN'T YA?

Shortly after American linguists Frank and Charlotte Mecklenburg arrived in New Guinea, a linguistic survey was planned to verify the language people spoke in the region of Olsobip—south of Telefomin at the foot of the Owen Stanley Mountains and close to Irian to the west and the Papua border to the south. It was the language of the community that Mecklenburgs believed God was leading them to serve. Walt Steinkraus, who lived and worked in nearby Tifalmin, was most familiar with the area and agreed to accompany Frank to carry out the survey on foot. But getting Frank and Walt from Ukarumpa to the region nearly three hundred miles distant was my job.

Nine months previously I had flown over that area, participating in an intense air search for a Missionary Aviation Fellowship Cessna 185, registered as VH-MFG, which had disappeared. That June 1967 morning, MAF pilot John Harverson had said good-bye to his wife, Joan. Another MAF pilot on the search told me that Joan believed she would never see her husband again after they parted that morning.

Did the Holy Spirit reveal this to her?

Jim Entz accompanied me in the Aztec, and we flew to Telefomin to assist in the search organized by the Department of Civil Aviation. They had assigned a controller to Telefomin to oversee the search operations for VH-MFG and Harverson, which was ongoing for two weeks. None of the twenty-seven pilots engaged in the search knowingly saw any sign of Harverson or the wreckage of VH-MFG in that rugged terrain.

MAF's accident report of VH-MFG, as found in *Balus Bilong Mipela* by Vic Ambrose, provides a description of the area:

> The route from Telefomin to Olsobip, 20 miles to the southwest, lies over a bad area, demanding a climb from almost 5,000 feet to cross the notorious Hindenburg Wall (the near-vertical escarpment separating Highlands from the Papuan Lowlands) at 9,000 feet, then a descent to Olsobip (elevation 1,200 feet) in the southern foothills of Papua. The Hindenburg Wall marks the junction of two weather areas and is nearly always tricky—the direct distance between the two places is only 17 miles, yet we have never flown it in less than 13 minutes and an average trip takes 40 to 50 minutes. (119)

When I related to the onsite DCA search controller the story of Harverson's wife somehow knowing she would never see her

YOU WERE SCARED, WEREN'T YA? 39

husband again, he said, "If that's true, we might as well call off the search." And that's what he did.

Having flown five hours in that search, I believed I was familiar enough with the area to schedule myself to fly Walt and Frank to start their survey. Rope, tackle, grappling hooks, shoes with steel cleats, and gloves were among the equipment Walt and Frank had packed. It was obvious they were prepared for some serious trekking. Everything was loaded into VH-SIB, our new, turbocharged Cessna 206.

First we flew to Telefomin, at an elevation of four thousand feet near the western border. From there, solid cloud coverage extended to the south. So to be safe I topped off our tanks from SIL's Telefomin fuel cache. We got airborne again and headed south for Olsobip, climbing en route, and crossed the nine-thousand-foot east-west stone ridge called Hindenburg Wall, fifteen miles to the south. I then looked for cloud holes to descend farther through the multiple cloud layers. Olsobip, at an elevation of 1,200 feet, was still more than a mile underneath us, located three miles beyond the foot of that wall and adjacent to a ninety degree turn of the Upper Fly River.

Because of multiple cloud layers extending farther south, it was necessary to go well south of Olsobip in order to descend, find the Fly River, and then do a 180 and follow the river north back to Olsobip. Upon reaching a 4,500-foot altitude, a dark thunderstorm and high cliff sides of the Fly River Valley forced us to do another 180, heading north sooner than I had wanted.

By then a second storm, dark with rain, had formed over the river in the direction we were heading—hence, danger in front and behind.

I had been calling Wewak control about every five minutes—maybe oftener—for weather reports of this area, but they had none. The river channel turned west, but Olsobip airstrip, which I thought would be at that turn, was nowhere in sight. Were there two rivers? Had I been following the wrong river? The air charts were not accurate. I was now unsure of our actual position. In the deteriorating weather, further flight in search of Olsobip was not wise.

At an altitude of 2,500 feet, hemmed in by storms in front and behind and high vertical banks on both sides of the river, I began climbing through rain and cloud in a race track pattern over the valley. At eleven thousand feet, I put on an oxygen mask to avoid getting woozy in the rarer air and to remain alert. It took the better part of forty-five minutes to reach 13,500 feet altitude before I was confident we were above any nearby mountain peaks. We then headed north toward thinning clouds. It's worth noting that without the turbocharged engine, we could not have attained those altitudes with the weight that was on board, nor had that margin of safety with the extra altitude.

We searched for landmarks hidden by clouds. From that altitude, Walt identified the Sepik River, which then led us back to Telefomin. We landed, topped off the tanks again, and headed home. I felt defeated, however, in not reaching our destination and that I had failed Frank and Walt.

Several weeks later, while filing a flight plan in Wewak tower, one of the DCA controllers asked if I had been flying VH-SIB in the Olsobip area recently, asking for weather reports. I told him I had. He responded, "I could tell from your voice—you were scared, weren't ya?"

I nodded yes.

Hindsight is usually 20/20. Perhaps I should not have persisted so long and hard in trying to find Olsobip, but knowing the 206 was equipped with a turbocharger gave me confidence that if need be we could climb from the deteriorating weather to clearer, somewhat brighter sky overhead and return to Telefomin. The scare for me occurred on this flight when the Olsobip airstrip was not where the river turned and where I thought it should be, which meant I believed I was truly disoriented, possibly lost! However, when Walt identified the Sepik River, I realized I hadn't been lost—the map I'd had along was wrong.

Frank and Charlotte Mecklenburg eventually lived in Olsobip, putting that language into writing. A translation of the New Testament into that language was completed in 1995.

In May 2013, Frank and I exchanged e-mails. He remembers that flight quite well, saying he had told many people about it. His version suggested a difference in that we had climbed to fifteen thousand feet to escape the deteriorating weather in Olsobip.

Looking back, I now realize I hadn't memorized the terrain around Olsibip very well during the VH-MFG search. Instead I had been concentrating on looking for a downed airplane.

17

SORCERY, OR TURN YOUR BACK ON GOD?

In 1956, when New Zealanders Des and Jenny Oatridge arrived in PNG, they deliberately selected a small ethnic group, the Binumariens, to serve and live among, just a few miles north and east of Ukarumpa. The total number of these people had dwindled to 112 souls. At first, Des and Jenny believed the diminishing numbers were attributable to disease, wondering also if the elders had forbidden women to give birth to children.

But in a June 2012 e-mail, Des clarified:

> [The elders] realized the reason their women were not having children at the rate they should to save the tribe, and this was not because of ill health. So the leading men asked the women what they were doing to prevent pregnancy. The women lied and said they weren't doing anything. Sisia, the Tultul [government-appointed local authority], told me he held a cane and threatened to beat the women if they didn't tell him what they were doing. I'm not sure, but I think he landed a few blows before they began to confess what they were doing. They

described some drastic bush contraception, which had been taught them by some Markham Valley women [and] was very [effective].

The reason they gave for using this contraception was they wanted to avoid the effort and hard work [that] came to them when they bore children. They just wanted to be free to do their garden work and go hunting in the forest with their husbands without the burden of child minding.

That was fifty-seven years ago.

As Des and Jenny Oatridge continued learning Binumarien culture and language, they created an alphabet, and began putting that tongue into written form.

Des and Jenny also learned that Binumarien people feared the power of sorcery being worked on them by neighboring language communities and by the "traditional doctor" living in one of their villages.

It took two years for Des to complete the translation of a rough draft of the book of Matthew into Binumarien. The chief was his language helper. Des had skipped the first seventeen verses of the first chapter.

On June 27, 2012, he e-mailed me:

The reason for this was that I found the genealogy dry and uninteresting myself, so I started at verse 18 and went on till we finished the book. The chief was extremely interested in all we translated and drew my attention to several things I had not noticed.

At the completion of the book, I told the chief apologetically that we should do the first 17 verses of chapter 1 so that we could say we have completed the book. He agreed, and when we had done verses 1 to 17, he showed no emotion but insisted that I bring the 17 verses up to the house above our village that evening, where there was to be an important meeting.

At about 6:30 p.m., I took two small kerosene-burning hurricane lanterns and Matthew 1:1–17 and went up to the house concerned, where people, mostly men, were gathering for the meeting.

The elders sat me down on the floor of the largest room by the fire, which was in the center of the room where all the big men sat facing across the fire toward the door. They sat there so they could see out the door and observe the approach of any enemy who may be lurking and race out and attack them. So there I was, facing the fire and the door with all the big men at my back. The younger men moved up against the fire with their backs to the door, looking attentively at me. The chief told me to read what we had translated that day and then they would have their meeting. So I began to read the first verse of the genealogy and I noticed all the men in the room moving up close to the fire and looking with interest at the pages I was reading. Some moved in from outside, and others moved into the big room from the smaller side rooms, and as I read, the atmosphere in the room was tense and completely silent. I was a little nervous because of the tension but kept on reading till I had completed verse 17.

One elder who was sitting beside me raised his hand and moved it from side to side in the faces of the men on the other side of the fire and said, "This is what we have always wanted to know. Are the things written in the Bible the white man's myths, or are they fact? They have to be fact, because what myth carefully records family names down through history like this? Only fact does that!"

I was humbled because the part of this book that I had held till last, because I thought it might put the people off the book, was the very part that meant most to them and changed their attitude from thinking it was myth to believing it was fact. I learned something new that night too as I realized that no part of God's Word is there for nothing. Every word of it is there for a reason, even if it may be uninteresting to me, and God's wisdom was greater than mine.

Until then, no Binumarien ever "turned their back on God." Why? They had never known of a

trustworthy God. They would only turn their back
on someone they trusted.

In today's speak, one might say God had their backs. A 1990
census indicates the Binumarien population had increased to
360.

Question: how did that elder gain insight that only fact, not
myth, carefully records family names down through history?

18

DUNAS AND THE DOW JONES INDUSTRIALS

In 1966, while my parents, Arthur and Hulda, were visiting from the United States, SILers Dennis and Nancy Cochrane invited them and our family of four for a long weekend at Kelabo, the village where they lived and worked alongside the Duna to analyze and develop their language. The Duna were among PNG's most colorfully attired people on the island.

In a 185, I flew all us Glucks to Kelabo. Nestled among the Southern Highlands, Kelabo for me always seemed a challenge to find.

Dennis and Nancy were at the airstrip along with a crowd of Dunas when we landed. I shall never, ever forget the sight of the men wearing their carefully preened wigs and the women in their swaying grass skirts.

My father, a stockbroker, was walking alongside several of the older Duna men, who were carrying our baggage. Dad was telling them about the Dow Jones Industrials and how the stock market worked—in English, of course. The men walked alongside - grinning, smiling, nodding, vocalizing obvious approval in welcoming their new visitors, especially the ones with grey hair – my father and mother! It only encouraged him to talk more rapidly and in greater detail. Walking behind them watching their excitement and listening, it was hard to contain myself and not guffaw.

Who had taught the Duna to be so friendly and hospitable, anyway?

A July 21, 2013, e-mail from Dennis reads:

> I still smile at the remembrance of your controlled crash landings at our airstrip. I mean, you often hit the runway pretty hard and bounced high a time or two before getting the plane firmly on the ground. I'm sure you remember me telling you how my kids noticed your landings, and when they landed their little JAARS model planes, they bounced them several times when landing, apparently thinking that was a normal way to land planes.

19

BUT ONLY HALF THE
AIRSTRIP AVAILABLE?

A cargo flight was scheduled for the Cochranes at Kelabo. I heard Dennis's voice on the hangar radio reporting that the weather there was fine, but only half of the airstrip was available because the villagers had decided to do maintenance on it. In light of that, he wanted to know if I would still fly that day. I radioed that I would try it, but if landing appeared too dicey, I would drop off the cargo at an airstrip nearby. The Kelabo airstrip length was already minimal, and with only half that length available, landing would be more than a challenge, taking off more so.

In retrospect, I should have said, "No, it's too dangerous. Let's reschedule."

While en route, I pulled out of my shirt pocket a small Berkeley version of the Bible and read the third chapter of Proverbs. Verse twenty-five said: "Do not be afraid when overcome by sudden fear." Those words put my mind at ease as I continued on to my destination.

On arrival, I flew over the airstrip to get a good look, pleasantly surprised to see that the whole length was available, but only half *the width*! Landing turned out to be a slam dunk, though not literally on touchdown.

How is it that verses from God's Word can so forcefully impact one's thinking, state of heart, and mind? To me it's a wonderful mystery!

20

THE IN-FLIGHT REPAIR

Mr. and Mrs. Jewell, parents of one of my Pittsburgh high school chums, had come to New Guinea to visit a young couple they were supporting financially. I flew them from Lae to Agaun, where John and Elizabeth Murane and their two young daughters, Marianna and Suzanne, were living among the Daga language community. It is close to a two-and-one-half-hour flight on a southeast track from Lae, which basically parallels the eastern coastline of New Guinea. Agaun is nestled in a valley of the Owen Stanley Mountains, due east of Port Moresby. The Jewells spent the night with the Muranes.

The next day I returned to fly the Jewells back to Lae. They said their good-byes and climbed into the 185. I radioed Moresby air control that we were taxiing at Agaun for takeoff with destination of Oro Bay. Moresby acknowledged, and soon we were airborne.

In PNG, normal aviation radio procedure for flights outside of air terminal control areas is to transmit "taxiing for takeoff" with the name of destination and then, after getting airborne, to transmit departure time with destination ETA to air control. After landing, then the actual arrival time is transmitted as well.

I tried transmitting our departure time to Moresby, but without success. Within five minutes, Moresby control began calling to ask if we were still on the ground or airborne. I tried answering, but the mic button was not springing back. The radio was not transmitting, and because the mic button was not springing back after I held it down to transmit, I suspected a defective button spring.

At my request, Mr. Jewell, sitting beside me, cupped his hands. While holding the flight control wheel steady with my knees and looking outside frequently as we flew east to exit the narrow Agaun Valley, I used my little pocket screwdriver to dismantle the mic. He watched as I put screws and other parts into his hands, shaking his head and smiling. The mic button spring was indeed broken. I stretched out the longest piece, doubling its length, reinserted it, and then reassembled the mic. We could transmit once more, and I radioed confirming our actual Agaun departure time with an ETA of Oro Bay to Moresby control.

After flying forty minutes northwest along the coast, we landed at Oro Bay, an old WWII airstrip on the east coast, to refuel. The parking area was an asphalt basketball court that American forces had no doubt constructed during the war. I climbed up on the wing strut with the fuel hose to refuel the wing tanks while Mr. Jewell worked the wobble pump handle back and forth. But, alas, no fuel was coming out of the nozzle. The pump had lost its prime. Using a crescent wrench kept in the plane, I unbolted the wobble pump, drained some fuel out of the plane wing tank sump, and poured it into the pump. Quickly I reconnected the pump and moved the wobble handle back and forth, which re-primed the pump.

With Mr. Jewell's help, the plane fuel tanks were topped off, and we continued on our way to Lae. After we landed and before he and Mrs. Jewell entered a taxi, they both thanked me, and Mr. Jewell commented, "I never realized the job you fellows do." He meant, I suppose, that he didn't realize the flying we did required dealing with other stuff—unexpected contingencies like a broken mic, a fuel pump that lost its priming, replenishing fuel into the plane tanks, and the ordinary tasks necessary to fly safely. He then wished God's blessings on us.

It is worth noting that for years, the Jewells met monthly for Bible study and prayer with my parents and about five other couples living in the Pittsburgh, Pennsylvania, area.

Of these couples, at least four of their children, myself included, have used our lives to serve in some mission capacity in Colombia, Brazil, Ethiopia, Pittsburgh, New Guinea, Cameroon, more recently, Zambia (Jim and Ellie Jewell). In November 2013 Jim and Ellie paid us a visit. He corrected me, stating, "Zekie, there were at least 10 of us if not a dozen of us (kids) who used our lives in some mission capacity." (Zekie was name Jim started calling me in hi school days.)

Were those regular times of Bible study and prayer by these parents just coincidental when it came to their children's choices of life service?

21

A LIGHTED MATCH
DROPPED INTO AVGAS

One morning, I unwound the long fuel hose from its neatly wound position to begin fueling the twin-engine Piper Aztec in preparation for the day's first flight. I topped off the right outboard tank, then the right inboard tank, and then the left inboard tank. While I had been refueling, a passenger had been watching and engaging me in conversation. That person left as I finished filling up the third tank.

As I began filling the fourth and final tank, my attention was drawn to the sound of the avgas splashing into the tank. I cannot explain why my curiosity was aroused. Normal 100/130 octane avgas splashing into a fuel tank sounds, to me, similar to that of eggs scrambling. It was a sound I'd grown used to hearing over the past three years when fueling planes. But this time the splash sound seemed just a tad different—somehow not so "splashy" sounding. Had viscosity of the fuel been altered? I couldn't tell, except it didn't sound quite like eggs scrambling—maybe more like the bubbling sound of boiling water instead?

I pulled the nozzle out of the tank and ran some through the fingers of my left hand onto the ground. It smelled right, just like avgas, so I continued adding more. The amount in this fourth tank was still low when I decided to stop fueling. Curiosity had gotten the best of me.

I had to know for sure if something was wrong and hollered to Jim Entz in the hangar, requesting a clean glass container. He brought a glass jar to me. With the jar in one hand and the fuel hose nozzle in the other, I walked away from the plane and filled the jar with fuel. Holding the jar up against the clear sky, I looked at it. The liquid was clear, quite pretty actually, the color of it being the correct aqua blue-green of 100/130 octane. Still I was not satisfied. Placing the jar on the ground, I lit a match and threw it into the jar as Jim watched. I shielded myself, expecting a ball of flame. Instead, the match immediately flamed out.

Jim informed me he had just transferred a fresh shipment of fifty-five-gallon drums of fuel, trucked up from Lae, to the underground fuel storage tank by the hangar. I had just pumped close to 250 gallons of *water* into the Aztec fuel tanks.

Jim saw that I was shaken emotionally and helped me walk back to the hangar, where we gave thanks to God.

If I had continued as scheduled and started the day's flying, there would have been just enough pure fuel in the fuel lines to start the engines, taxi to the end of the airstrip, and get off the ground before both engines would have quit. It was the sound of the splash that had caught my ear. An accident had been averted. Thank you, Lord, for the gift of a musical ear and acute hearing. But questions linger.

Whoever pays attention to the sound of fuel splashing, anyway? Lord, was that your spirit filling mine with curiosity? How can one know when to satisfy curiosity?

* * *

Note

That morning, the three other SIL aircraft—a 185, 206, and Hughes 300 helicopter—were to be refueled next from the same underground tank. By God's grace, multiple accidents and fatalities were avoided. Remember, I hadn't discovered it minutes earlier because my attention had been diverted as I was talking with someone while I replenished the first three fuel tanks. In hindsight I should have given my complete attention to the task at hand.

That incident raised a question: how often over the past fifty years have I missed receiving vital information because my attention had been diverted or divided?

The above scenario is somewhat similar to one that preceded an accident in 1972 involving this same Piper Aztec airplane when someone's attention was diverted. For the full account, see chapter eighteen of Jamie Buckingham's book *Into the Glory* (Logos International: 1974).

22

JIM, I'M ALL RIGHT NOW

It was roughly a two-and-one-half-hour flight in the 185 from Aiyura and down the Markam, Wau, and Garaina Valleys to Sila, an airstrip on the western slope of nearby Mount Lamington. To my knowledge, it is the only sloped (seemed like 10 percent) PNG airstrip with a dogleg on the top end. Jim and Jaki Parlier were dependent on SIL's flight service to this area where they lived in a Manalagasi community. Before the Sila airstrip was built, it was a ten-hour walk from the nearest airstrip, and few outsiders had been in that region.

Jim told me that on one occasion, while he was seated around a campfire at night in his shorts listening to stories of the past with several of the older Manalagasi men, one of the older cannibals took hold of the backside of the lower muscle in Jim's leg and said for all to hear, "Mmm . . . this would be good for eating."

The availability of air service to Sila stimulated the local economy, shortened the Parlier's walk to less than one hour, and simplified their living. One of the items Jim purchased to hasten literacy in the area and had flown to Sila was a Honda 90 trail motorcycle.

In one of their newsletters, I read that the Parliers had been in PNG since the early 1960s and had been engaged in the study and development of the Manalagasi Language since then. In 1974, they completed the translation of the New Testament into the Manalagasi tongue but had seen little evidence of any changed lives.

In 1975, they returned from needed R & R in the U.S. to New Guinea and Jim returned to the village alone. While riding his Honda to the village from the Sila airstrip, he was stopped by a young boy Jim knew, who asked to ride along. Sitting behind Jim on the bike, the boy said, "Jim, I'm all right now."

"What do you mean?" Jim asked.

As he put his hand on his chest, the boy said, "I've got Jesus inside me now, and when you get to the village, you'll see many others have Jesus inside too."

23

EWAPA—MY GADSUP FRIEND

Ewapa, an older Gadsup man, was employed as groundskeeper at SIL's child care center in Ukarumpa. He attended a weekly Bible study in our home for center employees, led by pilot Doug Hunt and me.

On one occasion I had been sick in bed for several days and heard a cough outside the bedroom window. Remember? Coughing is the polite way of announcing one's presence. Only thieves knock, and if someone answers, they run away. Ewapa was missing several front teeth, so his speech was a little hard to follow.

"Who's that istap?" I asked, in New Guinea pidgin for "Who's there?"

"Ewapa."

"Oh, Ewapa, yu com."

Ewapa opened the front door and came inside.

"Ewapa, yu com bak," I said, meaning to where I was—in the back bedroom.

Ruth and I had a simple house with pressed-paper board, similar to sheets of plywood, and painted interior walls. The first room he came to off the hallway was our bathroom. He asked what those basins were and how we used them. I explained that we washed our faces in the high bowl and the rest of our bodies in the real big bowl, and we didn't wash in the smaller, low bowl. He said slowly, "Ah, ntch, tch, tch," expressing surprise, wonder, and approval.

He walked slowly into the bedroom and stopped at Ruth's dresser, all the while exclaiming, "Ahh, ntch, tch, tch!" He opened each drawer and slowly said, "Ntch, tch, tch." He walked to the open closet, where our clothes were on hangers, slowly commenting, "Ntch, tch, tch."

Then he walked to my dresser and pulled open each drawer, still commenting, "Ah, ntch, tch, tch," as he looked. What he saw in the room, including the furniture and painted walls with two windows, I'm sure represented considerable wealth. Ewapa probably owned one pair of shorts and maybe two warm shirts, one of which he was wearing.

On the wall there was an oil painting of a lemon sliced in half above the headboard. He asked what it was. I explained it was a picture of fruit that grows in my homeland.

Then he climbed onto the bed with his bare, muddy feet and lay down alongside me with his legs still crossed. That must not have been comfortable, as he quickly sat back up and talked about his family and then mine. He mentioned his son in Port Moresby, asking if I could fly his son home, which I agreed to do if we could arrange it.

Then he said, *"Alrite, mi prea now."*

I have partially Anglicized his Pidgin English prayer.

"Oh, Papa God, tank you for my family; tank you for Mr. Ron and his family. Papa God, we live on the ground. But you are over everything. Papa, we know nothing. But you boss it all. Tank you, Papa God. Tank you too much.

"Now, Papa, before these people came, we didn't have your talk. It was like the sun was always shining. Our skin was always dry and hot; we were always scratching. But now these people have come and brought us your talk. It's like gentle dew, falling from on top, so soothing to our skin. We don't scratch anymore, Papa. Tank you, tank you too much, Papa.

"Now Papa, me ask, you put strong in Mr. Ron's body, you put strong in his legs, you put strong in his chest and arms, and good think-think in his head, and big strong in his bird (plane), and big, big strong in nose of bird (meaning propeller), and don't let it get sick and fall down and hit a rock or tree or something. Me ask, me ask, me ask in name of your pikinini Son Jesus—me ask. That's all."

He got down off the bed and walked out of the house. I didn't want to move. This humble man had prayed to God for restoration of my health in the name of God's Son, Jesus.

Questions: Where did Ewapa's concern for my health originate? Was it from the ongoing study and writing of his Gadsup tongue by SILers Chet and Marge Frantz? Was it the weekly Bible studies held in our home?

24

RABAUL CONTROL, CONTACT SIL!

Around 2:30 p.m. on a sunny afternoon in 1968, I was returning home a bit early from the day's scheduled flying in a 185, still about thirty minutes out from landing at Aiyura. Static on the HF radio frequency was loud, as it normally was at that time of day during the rainy season. Hearing and understanding any voice transmissions was next to impossible.

For kicks I switched over to a different air control frequency to hear what was going on elsewhere in the territory. Selecting 13.3 kilohertz, I heard more static. Suddenly the frequency went quiet, and I heard the strong voice of Harold Morton, a senior MAF pilot who was five hundred miles away, clear as a bell, urgently request Rabaul control to "contact SIL and tell them to get a plane out here to fly Jan Allen to the hospital in Lae."

His voice faded out, and loud static resumed. I could no longer understand anything. But when he said "Here," I knew Harold meant Buka Straits, adjacent to Bougainville Island. I switched to SIL's private radio frequency, called Uniform Whiskey, and requested our maintenance crew to top off the fuel tanks of the Piper Aztec twin, preflight it, and please get a message to Ruth that I'd not be coming home that evening.

The flight to Buka would be mostly over water, skirting the southern coast of New Britain, and take three and one-half hours. Around 3:00 p.m. I landed at Aiyura in the 185, made a pit stop, changed planes, and then took off for Buka in the Aztec, contacting Lae Control en route with my flight plan and then Rabaul Control when I was on the ground at Buka at six thirty. I had arrived a few minutes after sunset and would stay overnight before flying Jan to the Lae hospital the next morning. But I was unprepared for what happened next.

25

SWIMMING THE STRAITS

After parking and tying down the Aztec at Buka, I knew I needed a bath. The water in the straits alongside the airstrip, separating Buka from Bougainville, looked inviting. The place was deserted, and daylight was waning. With no one to tell, I put on my swim trunks and went into the water for a swim, not realizing how swiftly the water was flowing west to east. It carried me about thirty feet away from shore toward the middle. That did not upset me, as the water flow was slower where the straits widened, maybe seventy-five feet downstream.

To freshen up I ducked my head into the water, opening my eyes. The water was clear and I saw hundreds of nondescript, long fish lying on their sides on the bottom, perhaps eighty to one hundred feet below. At first I thought they were dead, but then I saw an occasional side fin move. It was getting dark, but my attention was hooked, and I looked one more time. My eyes were drawn to one of them swimming over the others—a shark. Suddenly I realized they were all sharks, big ones, and very much alive! I was shark bait and began swimming as hard as I could for shore, making little headway, before remembering to ask God for protection and strength. He enabled me to relax and swim slowly.

Finally my feet touched bottom and I walked out, not minding at all the thistles I stepped on during the long barefoot walk back to the plane in the moonlight, grateful to be alive and for the light. Later I realized that if I had become a shark's meal, nobody would have known.

The morning's flight back to Lae with Jan was uneventful. It turned out that the medical doctor in Lae Hospital did not believe her illness would require the invasive procedure that a medical technician in training at Buka had wanted to undertake.

Questions and a Comment

1. Did the sharks not notice the human bait (me) splashing far overhead due to the sun having already set?
2. Or had someone shielded me from their sight?
3. Judgment was woefully lacking when I took that dip. Getting out of the water was one of those times when my mind was filled with thanksgiving and gratitude for blessings of life. Who is the source of those reminders, anyway? Lord, is that you?

26

LEVITY, BY THE BOOK

Copies of the airplane manufacturer's operational manual were normally kept in the back pocket of the right front passenger seat of each plane. The manuals were thin and within easy access from the pilot's left seat.

Occasionally, for a bit of levity, I would hand a manual to a passenger and ask him or her to turn to the section on landing, and then, when the destination came into view, I would have him or her read each step out loud. Involving passengers in landings, I thought, always removed any sense of boredom on their part and helped lighten the day of everyone in the aircraft.

"A cheerful heart is good medicine," (Proverbs 17:22 - New International Version)

But it also had the added effect of exposing passengers to technical factors they probably never thought much about. Frequently, after we had landed and parked the plane, they would hand the manual back, get out, and walk away, shaking their heads, laughing or smiling with some silly comment about my ability (or lack thereof) to inspire passenger confidence.

One passenger who didn't know me made it known to others on board that he didn't take kindly to the idea.

27

PET POSSUM COMFORTS PASSENGERS

Vonnie Steinkraus almost always got airsick during the two-hour flight between Aiyura (the government agricultural station runway we called home) and Tifalmin, even when the air was calm. Certain other passengers also would experience airsickness regularly, no matter how calm the air was or how gently I moved the flight controls.

I, too, had gotten airsick multiple times during pilot training in the US Air Force. Airsick-prone passengers, therefore, had my sympathy. Getting them to their destinations without their becoming nauseated became a personal challenge.

Ageno, Ruth's hired house help, gave me a pet possum. The four-legged critter was perfectly sized to hibernate in my shirt pocket during the daytime, with its curled tail hanging down outside. On flights with Vonnie or others prone to airsickness, I'd bring along the possum. He was clean and nocturnal.

After taking off, I would remove him from my shirt pocket and place him on top of the instrument panel. His slow crawl diverted passenger attention completely from air turbulence, rain, or other threatening weather. Anxiety and airsickness were frequently averted, his movements invariably distracting the passengers' attention enough to enable them to arrive at their destination without nausea or sickness.

***

In March 1971 Walt and Vonnie Steinkraus and their two young daughters were buried in a half-mile-wide mudslide at Tifalmin, that also killed ten villagers. On an envelope recovered in the debris, the following was in Vonnie's hand writing: "As the heavens are higher than the earth, so are my ways higher than your ways and my thoughts than your thoughts" (Isaiah 55:9).

28

PEACE LAUGHING

My pastor's comments in a recent sermon about joy resurrected an airborne conversation that occurred years ago in New Guinea.

The Nazarene Mission had booked a flight with SIL to transport its visiting US mission board superintendent from Banz, the group's training station in the Western Highlands, to Port Moresby, to catch an international flight back to the United States. I was his pilot to Moresby.

Other passengers were along, but I had him sit alongside me in the front, primarily because of his portly size—a weight and balance consideration—but also to chat. I had been thinking about Nehemiah's instructions in 8:10b, to stop weeping and celebrate ". . . for the joy of the Lord is your strength." (New International Version)

This generation of Jews in question was hearing for the first time the Law that God gave to Moses and had come under conviction for their ignorance and wrongdoing. What fascinated me then and now about this verse is the correlation between joy and strength.

I asked the superintendent how he would define joy. Without hesitation he said joy is "peace laughing" as the turbocharged engine smoothly powered us comfortably over ridges and between rugged eleven-thousand-foot peaks of the Owen Stanley Mountains. Slowly I eased back the throttle to begin our descent to Port Moresby. Our conversation never progressed to the correlation between joy and strength.

I'll never forget that dialogue or the vista of those rugged mountain peaks beside and under us and Moresby and the blue sea, miles ahead. What a gift!

29

TWO CHIEFS

In 1969 I flew our family of four to Pangia in Papua New Guinea's Southern Highlands, invited by Harland and Marie Kerr to spend the weekend with them and their two young daughters in the Wiru village where they lived. After we landed, a large throng of people came running to encircle the plane, and quickly, I shut down the engine.

Harland helped me unload and secure the plane. The Wiru people picked up our baggage and the supplies we'd brought along for Kerrs, carrying much of it on their heads all the way to the village—for them, an honor. Harland then pointed out two men who were maybe sixty feet away, wearing feathered plumes of bright headdresses, and told us to watch, explaining these men had been traditional Wiru enemy clan chiefs.

I turned, just in time to see two barrel-chested guys run quickly toward each other, bump chests, and then embrace each other in bear hugs, laughing loudly and slapping each other, bumping chests repeatedly!

Why this behavior? Harland and Marie had translated portions of the New Testament into the Wiru tongue. On hearing it read to them, both chiefs, separately, had confessed ignorance to God and, after seeking his forgiveness, asked him into their lives.

The result was a complete life change in both men. Previously enemies, they were now close friends. For them, genuine concern for the welfare and care of those for whom they were responsible replaced killing, deception, appeasement of spirits, and fear of sorcery.

The Kerrs told us that rain had not fallen for weeks and discreetly pointed to sunken chests of the people. The area was experiencing a drought, and people were short of food.

Nevertheless, being told of our visit in advance, they had planned a big "sing-sing" (celebration) in our honor. We watched them butcher several huge pigs weighing about six hundred pounds each and simultaneously start fires in shallow dirt holes in the ground. Rocks thrown into the fires became red-hot. Banana leaves were placed on top of the hot rocks, and fresh vegetables and chunks of pork were placed on top of the banana leaves. Then more banana leaves were placed over the food being cooked on the hot rocks, forming a pressure cooker that was in effect for the next fifty or so minutes.

The cooked food was delicious, but only now, forty-four years later, am I realizing the significance of the Wiru people's sacrifice of their meager food supply in our honor.

Why did they do it? Because we were part of the support team helping Harland and Marie turn (translate) God's talk into the Wiru tongue. They were so grateful to receive God's talk.

The two clan chiefs we'd seen earlier, I realized, exemplified an end result hoped for by every SIL language team. In retrospect, for me, the scene of feasting and celebrating the arrival of God's Word during a famine remains humbling beyond words.

30

A WONDERFUL CONFIRMATION IN TWO BAGS

In 1970 a change of assignment occurred. Ruth and I were asked to start an air transport program in West Africa, and it necessitated living temporarily in Waxhaw, North Carolina, at the JAARS Center.

My parents and my sister and her family of five were to visit us in June, and we looked forward to their visit. But feeding and entertaining them was more than we could handle financially. We were living in a small house trailer, and our cash on hand consisted of change, except for one hundred dollars, which I had put aside to cover the birth of a new family member anticipated momentarily. I had not told anyone of our financial situation.

On the afternoon of June 7, Ruth, Cheryl, Sharon, and I returned from a meeting at the center. On the steps of our trailer were two large, full grocery bags containing frozen steaks, cobs and cobs of fresh corn, ice cream, and other goodies. There was more than enough food to feed our visiting family one complete meal, picnic-style outside under the tall trees.

Everyone I could think of to thank denied supplying the food. Ruth and I accepted it as God's provision to supply all our needs according to his promises, a wonderful confirmation.

That night in bed, Ruth awakened me; I drove her to the hospital in Charlotte, and in the early hours of June 8, Charles Arthur joined our family.

31

GOD, WASN'T THAT YOU—AGAIN?

Toward the end of our term in Papua New Guinea, I flew some American visitors to Manus Island, located about one hundred miles north of PNG across the Bismarck Sea, and was invited to join them for lunch in the home of the American missionary couple being visited. The table was amply prepared with food, and afterward I knew I had consumed more than I should have.

That afternoon, my passengers climbed back into the plane for the return flight, and we were soon airborne, headed for home. Both Aztec Lycoming engines powered us in a smooth climb over waters of the Bismarck Sea. I set the altitude control to climb to and maintain ten thousand feet on a southerly heading. The air was smooth, the day was sunny, and the sky was clear. It was CAVU—clear and visibility unlimited.

In the Piper Aztec twin, when propeller rpms are in exact sync—that is, both props are turning at exactly the same number of revolutions per minute—they elicit the smoothest of mechanical purring sounds. The passengers had stopped talking and fallen asleep. There was no radio chatter and I, with full tummy, was also finding it extremely hard to remain awake.

Some twelve or fifteen minutes later, I awakened. We were still maybe thirty miles distant from the mainland. The plane began going in and out of thin stratus clouds, but there was no sign of any other air traffic and certainly no mountains to worry about while over the water. The smooth air, heat of the sun, and purring of the engines was a soothing combination and very, very hard to resist. My eyes closed again for I don't know how long—maybe six or eight minutes.

A gentle air pocket caused the plane to drop slightly, enough to awaken me, and the vista ahead got my attention quickly. We had just crossed the coast and were now over the main island and within minutes of entering a towering cumulus cloud that had a hard center—namely, Mount Wilhelm, with a 14,700-foot peak. I made a gentle turn to a more direct route for home and began a slow descent. Before long we were on final approach and on the ground, home at Aiyura.

Now, in my eighty-first year, recalling that return trip in 1969 from Manus, I've been thinking . . .

1. God, wasn't that you, again, using a gentle air pocket to awaken me?
2. Had fatigue been entering my mind and body after nearly five years of landing in tropical temperatures, then taking off and climbing up to cool temperatures,

and then going back down to tropical ground temps, repeatedly, been taking a toll?

3. Were you reminding me, *again*, that simple choices like overeating have consequences?"

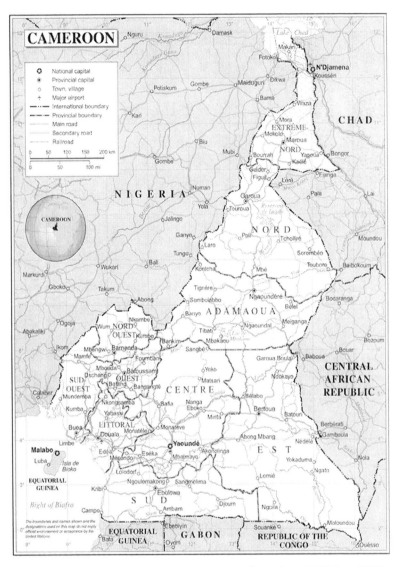

Cameroon, Africa Sept 1972 – May 1981 based on UN Map 4227

Cameroon

A change in our assignment from Papua New Guinea to West Africa required eighteen months of fund-raising in order to acquire an airplane, spare parts, tools, and shipment. In 1971, JAARS purchased a slightly used (three hundred hours) Cessna U206 six-seat with a three-hundred-horsepower engine. I named it *Friendship of Pittsburgh* to honor friends in my home area who helped fund it. A graphic artist with the Isaly's Dairy (known widely at the time for its ice cream) in Pittsburgh, Pennsylvania, created Friendship of Pittsburgh decals, which he helped mount on each side of the engine cowling.

Nigeria was our destination. However, political events, civil unrest from the Biafra conflict, and a change in Nigerian visa policy resulted in a change of plans. SIL's new air service in West Africa would instead be based in Cameroon, the neighboring country sharing Nigeria's east border. This complicated logistics, because stuff already shipped---206 spare parts, maintenance equipment and our personal effects were sitting in customs in a Nigerian port, accumulating storage fees daily. The change also meant that we would need to learn to speak fluent French, as French and English are the two official languages of Cameroon. I was finding it hard to be a happy camper with this change.

Nevertheless, a little research revealed that Cameroon is a former Portuguese and later French colony, shares borders with six other African nations, was granted independence in 1960 and is slightly larger in area than the state of California.

More importantly, Cameroon's 270 ethnicities speak 270 mother tongues or national languages, the majority of which are unwritten.

There were already three SIL linguistic teams comprised of three young expatriate married couples, authorized by Cameroon's Federal University of Yaoundé to study and develop three of the 270 languages.

32

ARRIVAL IN YAOUNDÉ, BUT WHERE TO GO?

Long before embarking on this venture, I had "endured" five years of French language study in junior and senior high school and in college, never dreaming I'd ever use it. In addition, our family went to Besançon, France, in June 1972 for ten additional weeks of intense French language study before arriving in Cameroon. Poor Ruth, having had no previous exposure to French, had to start learning it from scratch. On September 10, 1972, we arrived at the international airport in Douala, Cameroon, but the onward flight to our destination of the capital, Yaoundé, that evening was canceled.

On arrival in Yaoundé the next morning, I realized how little French I had learned. How did one ask for a taxi, let alone tell the driver where to take us? We had no way to contact Ron and Rhonda Thwing, the SIL couple who were to meet us the previous evening. Nor did I know of any housing arrangements.

Thankfully, taxi drivers at the Yaoundé Airport were helpful. I asked in French if they knew of a mission guesthouse. They did, and two cabs were needed to take us and our baggage there, where we met the Thwings. It was exactly where we needed to be and was the first of many, many occasions in which we were recipients of Cameroonian friendliness and generous hospitality.

Question: was my study of French years earlier just another piece of the Creator's grand plan?

33

RON THWING UNDERSTOOD

On April 3, 2011, during an evening with Ron Thwing and his wife, Rhonda, he reminded me of a visit we made together to the Ministry of Transport early in 1973, seeking authorization to import and operate a Cessna 206 in Cameroon.

We were ushered into a small office space where some women secretaries were working. They were talking among themselves in Bulu while awaiting their boss, the Minister. In the 1950s, Ron Thwing's parents had served as Presbyterian missionaries in south-central Cameroon, and Ron grew up learning to speak Bulu, one of Cameroon's 270 languages.

The secretaries, of course, didn't realize he understood what they were saying. Ron grew increasingly uncomfortable, quite certain the nature of it was confidential, not intended for our ears. So he spoke casually to them in Bulu, alerting them that he had understood all they had been saying. They laughed in surprise. Immediately the atmosphere relaxed as Ron and I were deemed part of the extended Bulu family, even though I understood absolutely nothing in Bulu. They were in a jovial mood when we were introduced to the Minister, who also was of Bulu ethnicity. Written authorization to import and operate SIL's 206 in Cameroon was granted quickly by the Minister. A decision was made to base the air service in Yaoundé, the capital.

Was it also part of God's plan years ago for Ron Thwing's Bulu fluency to facilitate this approval, and so quickly?

34

ENGINE FAILURE, PASSPORT, AND TURNAROUND

In April of 1973 Jim Bone and another United Airlines pilot ferried the *Friendship of Pittsburgh* from Waxhaw, North Carolina, to Cameroon. They were delayed two days by a fuel leak and had it repaired at Gander, Newfoundland. From there, they took off for the thirteen-hour transatlantic part of the flight.

Approximately one hundred miles out over the water, after reaching cruise altitude, they began sequencing fuel selector valves to redirect the fuel feeding the engine from the wing tanks to the ferry fuel tank, which was installed behind them inside the cabin. After changing the fuel selector valves, the engine suddenly stopped, the prop wind-milled, and the plane dutifully slowed and began a gliding descent! The pilots quickly undid what they had just done, and the engine just as dutifully resumed normal firing again on all six cylinders. They then realized sequencing the fuel selector valves was a somewhat more complex task, and tried it again, this time following the written instructions carefully. Their second attempt worked. Jim included this exciting tidbit while explaining the two-day arrival delay. That's why his copilot had gotten off at Dakar, Senegal, and boarded a flight back to the United States in order to work the next day. Jim completed the ferry flight to Cameroon solo.

I went to Douala to take delivery of the plane and watched it land just ahead of a westbound Pan Am 707 that would soon be heading for New York. Walking out onto the tarmac, I introduced myself, greeting Jim. He pointed to the 707 excitedly, shaking his finger, saying, "That's my ride home. I've got to get on that flight in order to be at work in Chicago tomorrow morning!"

At that moment, Kiki, a young Cameroonian friend I knew who normally hung out at the Yaoundé Aero Club, appeared, offering to help. Taking Jim's American passport, Kiki disappeared for about ten minutes, and then returned with the passport. He had persuaded immigration officials to stamp it. Jim briefed me on the 206 performance and its quirks. Forty-five minutes after landing, he handed me the 206 papers and keys, boarded the 707, and was headed back to the United States on another transatlantic flight.

My children were disappointed Jim wasn't able to come to Yaoundé as originally planned. They had prepared and hung festive banners welcoming him to Cameroon.

The date was April 12, 1973, and now, forty years later, I am pondering two questions.

1. How was it that Kiki appeared when he did, uninvited, facilitating the stamping of Jim's passport by Cameroon immigration officials, and enabling his forty-five minute turnaround?

2. Who superintended the timing of the Cessna 206 and Pan Am landings at Douala?

35

FLYING A TRIBAL CHIEF

I flew the 206 to Yaoundé, where I was greatly relieved to discover my tools and toolbox, all 110 pounds of them, in the cargo pod underneath the plane. Without them I could not have removed the ferry tank, reconnected the fuel lines for normal flight operations, or maintained the plane.

My first SIL flight in Cameroon on April 19, 1973, was transporting two fifty-five-gallon drums containing the personal effects of SIL's Pat Peck to northwest Cameroon, landing on the Ndu Tea Estate airstrip. Pat and her coworker Lynne Fiore had moved to that area to study the Wimbum language.

While I was unloading the drums, someone introduced me to the local chief. I asked him if he'd like to ride in the airplane.

He nodded yes.

So I pointed out a seat for him, secured his shoulder and seat belts, and climbed in. We took off, circled slowly over the Ndu area, and then landed. He got out of the plane, and immediately his people surrounded him, very excited. He was delighted at the new and unexpected attention he was now receiving.

I flew back to Yaoundé and received a letter ten days later from an angry missionary I didn't know, who said, in effect, "You flew a tribal chief who practices sorcery and witchcraft! Why are you compromising the gospel?"

In answering his letter, I asked if people such as the chief were not the ones that God intended us to engage and serve.

36

WHERE ARE YOUR PEOPLE?

Not long after the flight program became operational, newly arrived SIL Director David Maranz and I were summoned in an announcement on Cameroon's public radio station to report to the Ministry of Territorial Administration. Upon arrival at the ministry, we were taken directly to the office of the Minister.

He was a tall, cordial young man who was dressed in a long robe and a fez and spoke excellent English. However, he didn't mince words.

He noted that SIL was the only nonprofit expatriate group to import an airplane into the country. And he said he knew SIL was flying linguists to remote parts of Cameroon to study languages. "Where," he wanted to know, "are these personnel located in the country?"

Dave and I both hesitated in answering his question, each of us wondering what was behind it. Why did he really need to know? We just stood there, hemmed and hawed, finally explaining that the linguists were situated in out-of-the-way places so that the ethnicities they lived among could have God's Word translated into their mother tongues.

The minister got exacerbated and raised his voice. "Don't you think I am also engaged in God's work overseeing the country's security? Do you not realize my government has responsibility for the security of your people as guests of our government? Now, please—tell me where they are located!"

Dave apologized, both of us very relieved to know that the issue of security was why the minister wanted to have the locations. Dave saw that that information was promptly delivered to the minister.

In retrospect, how often do people in very high government positions view their authority as the work of God? In Cameroon, we were truly privileged guests of a hospitable government.

37

WHERE'S YOUR HUSBAND?

One of my early flights in Cameroon was to take Solomon Nforgwei to northwest Cameroon. The flight itinerary was to first drop off cargo at Yoko for the Thwings. The second leg would be directly west to Bamenda, Solomon's home area, where the American ambassador, an elderly man, would be waiting with his sister for me to fly them back to Yaoundé. The complete trip would take four hours of flying, and the Yoko–Bamenda leg would be an hour flying over patches of dense rain forest and grassland.

After landing at Yoko and offloading the cargo, I restarted the engine and revved it for the routine magneto check. Alas! One of the magnetos was not working. (Light aircraft engines like the 206 have two complete ignition systems, including two spark plugs in each cylinder and two magnetos, each magneto generating sparks to one of the spark plugs in each cylinder.) Flight with only one functioning magneto is unwise.

When I tried to radio my predicament, no one responded. I even tried transmitting on 121.5 megahertz, the international distress frequency, but no one was listening. And there was no way to alert the embassy or the ambassador.

So Solomon spent the night at Yoko with the Thwings, and I borrowed their car, drove back to Yaoundé, and returned the next morning with a spare magneto and tools to install it.

In the meantime, the US embassy in Yaoundé had been phoning our home. "Where's your husband? The ambassador has been expecting him."

Ruth replied, "I don't know, sir. He's not here."

"Well, doesn't his plane have a radio?"

She got about four or five calls from this man, who on the last call was beside himself, shouting, and then after a brief silence, he finally said, "My God. I'm yelling at the pilot's wife!" He then apologized.

The embassy was rightly concerned, not knowing the whereabouts of their ambassador. However, the ambassador did what I had done. He returned to Yaoundé with his sister using ground transport because I hadn't shown up.

As soon as I could, I called on him at the embassy to apologize. He laughed, saying he understood and then scheduled another flight with me.

38

LETTER: IT TAKES A TEAM

In 1978 in Cameroon I received an aerogram (a lightweight letter-envelope combination) from Helen Marten and Velma Foreman in Papua New Guinea. They had recently completed the translation of the New Testament in Yessan-Mayo and were inviting all who had had a part in that project to the dedication celebration. I was curious. Why had I been invited? I'd not had a part in that effort. It took awhile for my thinker to get in gear.

Well, yes, I had. From March 1965 to November 1969, I had flown Helen and Velma multiple times to and from Ambunti in the Sepik River area, where they would transfer supplies from the plane into a carved-out log canoe and motor up that alligator-infested river for several hours to the village where they lived and worked in Yessan-Mayo communities.

And whenever they would return to Ukarumpa for a break, my wife, Ruth, as center hostess, fed them and helped them settle into the guesthouse. So, yes, Ruth and I did have a minor support role in that translation project, and it was wonderful knowing that the Yessan-Mayo people could now read and hear God's talk in their mother tongue. Because of duties in Cameroon, however, we were unable to go to the dedication celebration.

In thinking more about that invitation, the number of folk who had a part in helping Helen and Velma achieve the Yessan-Mayo New Testament translation extended well beyond Ruth and me.

There were many others at Ukarumpa serving in supporting roles, in areas such as the printing department, the radio department (which maintained transceivers for communication and also tape recorders for language study and analysis), the center post office, the finance office, the construction department, the center store, and the aviation department, not to mention help from linguistic and translation consultants.

And then there were supporting churches and personal donors and all others who prayed for them back home and the administrative staff at the Wycliffe headquarters home offices who receipted and transferred funds and handled their personal affairs.

The total probably approached hundreds of people, many of them not even knowing Helen or Velma personally—a marvelously coordinated team of volunteers committed to the same task: assuring the translation of the Scriptures into mother tongues of minority ethnicities.

Question: what motivated everyone in those supporting roles, enabling it all to work together? Certainly it was not the incentive of the monthly financial support being received.

39

STRAWBERRY JAM

In April 1973 Ruth and I ended formal French language study at the French Cultural Center in Yaoundé, but we continued learning. She assumed the buyer and hostess roles for the new Cameroon SIL entity, while I concentrated on getting flight operations airborne. An SIL couple working in the northern Cameroon wrote a letter to us requesting strawberry jam on the next flight headed their way. Ruth searched and searched in Yaoundé, finally finding some that had been imported from Belgium. Since she didn't know when it would be available again, she bought a whole box, twenty-four small jars of it. On my next flight north, I flew the box of jam to them, along with mail and fresh meat. The meat they kept, but they sent the jam back. It wasn't the right kind of strawberry jam!

I'd forgotten how picky people could be about food they eat.

40

ANOTHER POWER:
MOKOLO—CAMEROON

In May 1973 I flew a passenger to Mokolo in Northern Cameroon to meet with veteran Swiss missionary Hans Eichenburger. After greeting us warmly, Hans then told the story of how he came to settle in Mokolo.

In the time period of 1946–1947, just after WWII, seeking guidance for ministry in Northern Cameroon and traveling as far north as Mokolo, Hans happened upon a group of local people. His white skin was somewhat of a novelty, and a gathering of curious local people, including a tribal chief, had surrounded him.

One of the men began talking and said, "Our chief has special powers. He can change himself into a lion."

Others in the gathering around Hans concurred, saying, "Yes, he does."

The first man continued, "He can make himself into a jackal."

"Yes, he does," the others chimed in.

"He can change himself into a green mamba," the first man said, referring to a poisonous snake.

"Yes, he does," said the others, nodding.

Then Hans said to them, "Well, I know someone who died and came back to life again."

The chief said, "We have never heard of anyone with that kind of power. Please stay and tell us about him."

Because of the chief's invitation, Hans settled there with his wife. Together they learned the language of their hosts, put it into writing, taught the people to read the language they spoke and served them for the greater part of their lives.

CAMEROON TRIBUNE NEWSPAPER ARTICLE

Several months after I heard Hans relate that bit of personal history, an article appeared in the English edition of the *Cameroon Tribune,* a government-owned weekly newspaper, which issued warnings to village sorcerers and traditional doctors in Southwest Cameroon to refrain from engaging in witchcraft—from changing themselves into alligators or other animals that killed people or caused them to completely disappear or to be encumbered in some way. If they didn't stop, they would face prosecution and incarceration.

Can you imagine the fear that could envelop a person who lived in such an environment, without the personal knowledge and protection of God's love? If you were in their shoes, wouldn't you also be trying to appease the spirits for protection?

I'M SO HAPPY. TIKAR IS MY LANGUAGE!

In 1974, newly arrived Carol Stanley of Canada and Ellen Jackson from Washington State, both linguists and single, decided to be partners on a language project. They studied Cameroon's language situation and agreed to assist the Tikar-speaking communities in central Cameroon in developing the Tikar language—that is, analyzing the language, creating an alphabet, and writing Tikar to start with. All that was needed for them to start was government authorization.

A new agency of the government had just been created—ONAREST, the National Office of Science and Technical Research, to which SIL had just become accountable. Research authorization from ONAREST would be needed in order for Carol and Ellen to study the Tikar language.

I accompanied Carol and Ellen to see the director of ONAREST, introducing the ladies and myself to him and explaining in my very best French (which really was quite poor) what the ladies were hoping to do.

In perfect English, he responded, "What language do they want to study?"

"Tikar," they told him.

"Oh!" he said. "I'm so happy. Tikar's my language!"

Immediately he summoned his secretary and dictated a letter that she typed on government letterhead, authorizing Carol and Ellen to undertake the study of Tikar. While the secretary was typing his letter, he began teaching Tikar greetings and some vocabulary to Carol and Ellen.

About forty-five minutes later, the three of us left with a letter of authorization in hand for Carol and Ellen to undertake research of the Tikar language and culture, which under the previous system could have taken a month or more to obtain.

The director of ONAREST being Tikar—was it only a coincidence? It couldn't have been a God thing, could it?

43

LIGHTNING SEEMED EVERYWHERE

In early 1980 I agreed to do a charter flight, transporting the German foreign agricultural aid group CEENEMA to Foumban. It was a one-hour flight directly north of Yaoundé. The rainy season had begun, but I had agreed on the condition that the passengers return to Foumban in time for a 2:00 p.m. departure back to Yaoundé in order to escape the heavy afternoon seasonal rains that were just starting.

On arrival at Foumban, the CEENEMA people dispersed to do their business, and I sat in the plane doing paperwork, awaiting their return.

But my estimate of the timing of the afternoon rainstorm was way off. By 1:00 p.m., the wind had already picked up, and just to the north, huge, billowing dark clouds of red dust, embedded with flashes of lightning, were blowing south toward Foumban. Rain would arrive much earlier than two o'clock. Concerned, I looked for a way to tie down the plane, but there was only a tree nearby. It's hard to secure a plane to a tree, and there were no cement tie-downs to secure it to the ground.

Fortunately, my passengers showed up just then, having also seen the storm approaching, and clambered into the plane. They brought one extra person, the German ambassador, asking if there was room for him. I agreed, but since he was the smallest of the group, I directed him to a rear seat because of aircraft weight and balance considerations.

Interestingly, while climbing into the plane, the ambassador asked me, an American, if we could still be friends in spite of then President Jimmy Carter's announced boycott of the 1980 Olympics. I assured him we could.

Starting the engine, I taxied to take off to the south, with strong tailwinds blowing from the north, in order to avoid flying into the turbulence of the approaching storm. I could not hear instructions from the tower controller. Noise from the heavy rain already falling onto the control tower's metal roof drowned out the controller's departure instructions.

Fortunately, the airstrip was 4,500 feet long—our takeoff roll before liftoff was very extended with the forty-plus-miles-per-hour wind on our tail.

In the air, we found ourselves in the cusp of the leading edge of brutal turbulence, vicious rainsqualls, red dust, and bright, blinding lightning flashes that seemed in every direction. Loud thunderclaps drowned out all other sounds. I maintained a south heading toward home, flying beneath the cloud base with two to three miles of visibility in rain, which slowly improved as we gradually outpaced the storm, also heading south. Static on the radio was horrible, but in between bursts of it I could hear the voice of my friend Kiki, now a Cameroon airline pilot. He had just taken off at Douala, farther south on the coast, reporting thunderstorms in the whole area.

I maintained an altitude of just a few hundred feet above ground, beneath the low cloud base, going around hills of higher elevation, but always reverting back toward the southerly direction of our destination, Yaoundé.

After twenty minutes in the air, most of the hilly region was behind us, and we were in smoother air. For a few moments I found myself questioning the decision to depart Foumban. Had I just put my life and those of these five men at risk? Was it just "get-home-itus"? If I had not taken off, we would have been safe, I thought, but would have also likely lost a $60,000 airplane, blown to who knows where and damaged beyond repair. To me there were no good, easy answers.

About thirty-five minutes after takeoff, I began hearing transmissions from the Yaoundé control tower on static-free FM radio. I gave them our ETA and requested a report of local weather. They reported heavy rain in the east, west, and south sectors and that the north, the direction from which we were approaching, was gradually deteriorating but was still above minimums for VFR flight. We were instructed to continue and to report on final approach.

The rain was gradually increasing. (Thank you, Lord, for that reliable engine. It never misfired as the propeller pulled us through heavy rain.) The lightning had tapered off. We followed the road to Yaoundé, and the airport south of town came into view. A few minutes later I reported, "Echo Uniform on final." The tower asked me to turn on my landing lights so they could see the plane, which I did. The tower then cleared us to land. Touching down in heavy rain, I coasted up to the terminal to let out my passengers. They got soaked running into the terminal. We had actually landed a few minutes earlier than my ETA because of help from the north wind blowing us home.

I then taxied back to the other end of the runway, to SIL's rented hangar space at the aero club. After shutting down the engine, I climbed out with the hand-steering bar, fastened it to steer the nose wheel, and began pulling the plane, turning it into position to push it backward into the hangar. But the gentle incline to the hanger entrance was too steep. The aero club hangar custodian saw my distress, ran outside, and helped push. Just as we got the plane inside, the heavens opened up, and it rained like I had never seen before. The noise of it pounding on the corrugated metal roof was deafening. I waited there for close to two hours. When the rain subsided, it was dark, and I rode my little Honda 70 motorcycle home in foggy drizzle.

Ruth knew something had happened, because I was quiet. After eating dinner and helping put the kids to bed, I described the return flight home. She handed me a letter that arrived that day from a Swiss colleague and fellow JAARS/SIL pilot, Hans Stahli, who was home in Switzerland at the time. One sentence of all that he had written stood out: "Dear Ron, each night before going to sleep, I pray for you." Then I understood.

Is there a better reminder of the importance of the prayers of God's people than being on the receiving end of his love and protection?

A DARK STRIPE—OR TOILET PAPER FILTERS

In July 1975, before taking a USAID charter flight, a fifty-hour engine inspection was due on the 206 engine, which essentially meant an oil and filter change. At my request, JAARS had installed an additional oil filter on this engine before it was ferried to Cameroon. The filter had been recently approved by the US Federal Aviation Agency for light aircraft.

The new filter design was simple. The filtering element was a roll of good-quality toilet paper, which collected dirt from the oil flowing through it under pressure. (Several years earlier I had installed one in my car, and it worked wonders. The engine oil in my car was very dirty. Initially I changed the TP frequently, because it got dirty so quickly. But the TP did remove dirt so well that before long the engine oil looked as clean as pure honey. There is no better way to prolong the life of an internal combustion engine than to use clean engine oil.)

After the regular and TP filters were changed, Hans Staehli started the engine to check for oil leaks. None were visible, so we replaced the cowling, boarded our USAID passengers, and took off, Hans serving as pilot-in-command in the left seat and I in the right copilot seat. As he advanced the throttle forward, the plane accelerated down the runway and became airborne.

For some reason, the adjustable right front seat where I was seated had been positioned to the lowest setting, too low for me to see out front, and my shoulder harness restrained me from bending over to reach the seat crank, so I watched the engine gauges staring me in the face and noticed the oil pressure gauge didn't get much above forty pounds per square inch. With cold engine oil, normal takeoff oil pressure should have indicated sixty pounds per square inch or slightly higher. As Hans continued the climb out from takeoff, the oil pressure, in fact, was decreasing rather quickly.

I told Hans, "We've got a problem—decreasing oil pressure. Reduce power, turn around, and land ASAP." He radioed Yaoundé tower that we had an emergency and were returning to land. They cleared us for an immediate landing.

As we got close to the ground on final approach, a dark narrow stripe parallel to the runway centerline became visible. It was oil that had leaked from our engine. The only redeeming factor was that the stripe was exactly parallel to that white line, indicating a straight take off! If Hans had not reduced power and landed right away, the engine, within minutes, would have stopped because of oil starvation, and we likely would have crash-landed in rainforest.

Lord, was that you who arranged for the copilot seat to be cranked low, positioning my eyes directly in front of the engine instrument gauges?

The TP oil filter and hose installation, unfortunately, was also a safety hazard. Because it was installed outside the engine block, oil under pressure flowed out of the crankcase through a hose to the TP canister. Filtered oil then returned in another hose back into the crankcase. If the canister or hoses were not properly secured, oil leakage occurred. In this case, the canister had not been properly secured after inserting a clean roll of TP.

Later, after getting the USAID passengers to their destination, we returned to Yaoundé. Hans then removed that filter and the external hoses from the engine, thus eliminating the possibility of future occurrences.

In retrospect my judgment had been unwise. It was unsafe having the TP filter installed on an airplane engine in the first place.

International Relations: Washington, DC, and New York

July 1981—April 2007

Promoting Effective Cooperation and Goodwill between SIL, Governments, and the International Community

A New Compass Heading

Living in Arlington, Virginia, just across the Potomac River from Washington, DC, simplified the daily commute in our assignment with SIL's international relations team in DC. Besides, the concept of relating to governments of countries hosting SIL personnel and keeping them informed of language developments "back home" helped to enlist their collaborative support—which also helped minimize visa issues. Creativity and budget were the only limiting factors in this assignment. The increasing educational need of our children was added inducement to remain stateside. For all practical purposes, flying days were over.

Diplomats are posted to other countries to represent and promote the interests of their own governments. Two locations in the United States desired by foreign diplomats are Washington, DC, to the US government and New York City to the United Nations. Some countries can afford only one embassy, usually in New York.

Like anywhere else, promotions in diplomatic circles mean increased authority—with an exception. Several current heads of state previously served as ambassadors to the US government, including the ambassador of one West Africa country to the United States, a personal friend. He was summoned home to become prime minister.

45

SIL OFFICE IN WASHINGTON, DC

Ed Davis, an American, worked for the Organization of American States and traveled frequently to the capital cities of South America, where he first learned of SIL. On one of his Mexico City stops he met SIL founder Cameron Townsend and told him that most capital cities in the Americas had an SIL office. Why not establish one in Washington, DC?

Townsend explained he would like to but simply did not have the budget. Besides, he added, SIL only had relations with foreign governments only, not the United States Government. So in the 1960s, Ed and his wife, Elizabeth, completely sold on SIL's unique mission and purpose, had a red-colored phone installed in the kitchen of their Arlington, Virginia, home. That phone was listed under the name of SIL (Summer Institute of Linguistics at the time, now SIL International). In due time, others assumed responsibility to fund an SIL office in downtown DC. Initially the office was largely staffed by local volunteers. Early in the 1970s, Wycliffe provided budget, and personnel were assigned to the DC SIL office.

In March 1975, SILers John and Carolyn Miller and their daughter were captured in Vietnam. Negotiations for their release were initiated through SIL's Washington, DC, office. The Millers' release occurred seven and a half months later.

46

BRIBERY OR FRIENDSHIP?

A young employee of an embassy in Washington, DC, handled applications and other paperwork for visas and stamped them into passports. She was also the embassy receptionist and barely cordial the first few times I came to the embassy, probably because I always came for the purpose of getting visas—which meant more work for her.

In the early 1980s, shortly after meeting her, she phoned me at the SIL office to tell me of a letter complaining of visa service that SIL personnel sent to her boss, the ambassador. She told me that because of that letter, she could lose her job. There was no mistaking that she was upset.

In talking further with her, it was evident that she was not at fault. The SIL couple involved confirmed why they had complained to the ambassador. I then informed them how the process works and advised the ambassador to disregard the complaint, thanking him for the timely visa services always rendered by his visa officer.

On the receptionist's desk was a photo of three children, and she confirmed she was their mom. One of my next visits to the embassy was to retrieve some visas. In return for them I handed her a small bag of M&M's for her kids. From then on she could not do enough to help. On future visits to the embassy, as soon as she saw me, she would get up from behind her desk and come into the reception area regardless of others waiting there to give me a hug.

Was the little bag of M&M's bribery or a gift of appreciation for timely service?

47

YOU'VE NEVER EVEN MET YOUR OWN PRESIDENT?!

On a Friday evening in 1984 our phone rang in Arlington, Virginia. "Ron," the voice at the other end said, "this is Sol." He—Solomon Nforgwei—told me he was at the Four Seasons Hotel in nearby Georgetown, accompanying his president, who had come on a state visit to call on President Ronald Reagan.

I asked, "Have you already been to see President Reagan?"

"Yes, we had lunch with him at the White House yesterday."

"Well, what kind of man is he? I've never met our prez."

"You've never even met your own president?!" To me, a commoner, Sol's response seemed funny.

The next morning, Saturday, I drove to the Four Seasons, and we visited a few minutes. While I was with him, the room phone rang, and he was instructed to come downstairs for the drive to Dulles Airport and for his return flight to Africa. We prayed together briefly, and then, carrying some of his luggage,

I accompanied him downstairs, where we said good-bye as he entered the limo awaiting his president.

Driving home it occurred to me that his country was blessed to have such a godly servant so highly placed in the government.

48

LEOPARD SKIN AND COMEUPPANCE

In 1984, an American SILer in Peru sent a letter to the Washington, DC SIL office requesting help in having an enclosed document notarized by the Peruvian embassy. This second document was a request to export a leopard skin back to the United States. It angered me a little, because it seemed an abuse of our services. However, I complied with the request and walked it to the embassy, leaving the document with the consul-general, who assured me it would be ready the next day. But that next day the consul-general was out, and the document was not ready. I returned the third day and got the same story.

On the fourth day, I returned, and the consul-general was there. He explained that his wife had been ill and he had stayed at home to care for her, apologizing for his absence the previous two days. He then handed me the notarized document. In receiving it from him, I was abrupt in my thanks and left the embassy. While walking back to the office, I was suddenly overcome with guilt. The consul-general had done the right thing in staying home to care for his wife. I had not shown any sympathy or concern, not even asking if she was doing better or if I could be of help.

At that moment I vowed to return to the embassy at the next opportunity to apologize for my behavior and inquire about his wife's health. But I didn't get to it until four more days had passed. On arriving at the embassy, I asked to see the consul-general and was informed that he had returned to South America with his wife.

There was little I could do. But, I promised myself, that from then on I would listen to foreign embassy officials more closely and to personal concerns they might express, be it a health issue, concerns about aging parents back home, appropriate schooling in DC for their children, a troubling political issue their government was facing, etc. I would also offer to pray with and for them at the time.

After adopting that principle, I did not pray on every embassy visit, but when I heard a personal concern expressed, no official ever refused my offer to pray with them concerning their problem.

49

A NEW AFRICAN DIPLOMAT
AS ALLY IN DC

In 1992, I made a courtesy visit to welcome newly arrived Ambassador M. from West Africa to Washington. His handshake and appreciative response included a request to come see him if our colleagues working in his country ever experienced difficulty communicating with his country's government.

(This ambassador's initial welcoming statement and request illustrates a reason for SIL's office in Washington, DC. Keeping the officials of countries hosting SIL personnel regularly informed of progress and benefits occurring in such programs also helps achieve the mutual goals of SIL and the government—a primary one being increased understanding between national language ethnicities in the country and their national government.)

I e-mailed SIL's director in that country to advise him of the ambassador's offer, asking if they had any issues the ambassador might help alleviate.

The director replied, "Ask the ambassador if the visas the embassy issues could be for longer duration, so that our new personnel attending the three-month Africa Orientation Course would not miss the final few days."

When I raised that issue with the ambassador, he said, "I wrote the current regulation. Of course it can be changed!" A modified regulation was soon in effect, enabling visa applicants to request three- or six-month visitors visas.

While in his country I had learned a few greetings in Ewondo, the ambassador's mother tongue, and made it a point to use them when greeting him. From then on, whenever our paths crossed, he always tested me on *all* Ewondo greetings—for morning, noon, afternoon, and evening. Even when attending formal embassy functions where Ruth and I were in the reception line to greet him and his wife, he would hold up the line in order to test me on the greetings in his mother tongue and then smile broadly as if to say he and I had performed well.

Upon learning of completion of the Ejagham New Testament translation done by Ejagham speakers and SIL's John and Kathie Watters, the ambassador agreed to host a celebratory reception in his Washington residence. Ejagham-speaking university students in the Washington, DC, area and Ejagham speakers on the embassy staff attended, obviously delighted that their language and culture were being celebrated by their own government. They heard a few verses read from the New Testament in their mother tongue for the first time.

By Washington standards, the reception hosted by Ambassador M. at his residence was not attended by any major player of America's political arena inside the Capital Beltway. Instead, about sixty guests, most of whom were Africans, came to celebrate the completion of the translation of the New Testament into Ejagham—a language spoken by 140,000 people in southeastern Nigeria and in the Southwest Province of Cameroon—a project started in 1974.

Ayamba Nkiri, an Ejagham native speaker and guest of honor, told attendees how his mother had been baptized as a Christian into a local church and was able to recite the Lord's Prayer in perfect English but was unable to understand a word of it. Ayamba, at the age of thirteen, realized his people were experiencing a major communication problem in the church. The next Sunday he stood alongside the catechist, who was speaking in English, and translated everything into Ejagham. People came to him after that service expressing enthusiastic appreciation, because for the first time they understood what was being said in church. It was then that Ayamba believed he should help translate the Bible into Ejagham for his own people. Beginning in 1981, he worked alongside linguists John and Kathie on that project.

The translation was completed in early 1995, printed one year later, and soon afterward was presented to the Ejagham people.

Question: who gave Ayamba, at age thirteen, insight to understand that communication issue?

50

CAPITOL HILL BIBLE TRANSLATION DAY CELEBRATION

In 1967, a US Senate and House resolution officially designated September 30 as Bible Translation Day.

The Hanga language New Testament translation was completed in 1983. It is a language spoken in Ghana, where Geoffrey and Rosemary Hunt of the United Kingdom had led the translation effort. A senator from Colorado presided over the celebration of this achievement on Capitol Hill in September of that year.

A letter from then President Ronald Reagan was read, in which he encouraged and urged all Bible translation agencies to complete translations of the Bible into the remaining three thousand languages in the world without them.

Ghana's ambassador and his wife were guests of honor, along with the Hunts. Others in attendance included Capitol Hill staffers; representatives of Bible translation agencies; a dozen members of Congress; Elaine Townsend, the wife of SIL cofounder Cameron Townsend, recently deceased; David Cummings, president of Wycliffe; and local supporters. The celebration took place in caucus room 325 of the Russell Senate Office Building before a standing-room-only crowd.

After Senate Chaplain Dick Halverson read selected portions of the Scriptures, the Hunts were called to the front to be recognized. They gave a copy of the Hanga New Testament to our friend, the Ghanaian ambassador, which elicited sustained applause and cheering lasting for what seemed like several minutes. Witnessing elected leaders of the US government endorsing and cheering on the vital task of Bible translation brought me to tears. The occasion concluded with a prayer by a senator from Iowa. Invited guests then adjourned for a catered lunch in the Senate dining room. The luncheon was privately funded.

A complete transcript of this event is recorded in the *Congressional Record*, volume 129, number 133.

51

A NEW FRIEND AND ADVOCATE

Ambassador P. from West Africa arrived in Washington in 1981. Eventually he and his wife became very close friends with my wife and me. Shortly after the ambassador's arrival, my colleague Dave Witmer learned the date of the ambassador's birthday. Dave called a bakery near the office, ordering a large cookie. We delivered it to the ambassador. After lighting a candle in the center of the cookie, Dave and I sang "Happy Birthday" to the ambassador, much to his delight.

In 1984, on a Friday evening, I read a brief *Washington Post* news item telling of a coup attempt in the ambassador's country. Early the next morning, I drove to his residence in DC to see how he and his wife were doing. They were naturally upset about this event back home and accepted my offer to pray. I prayed simply, asking God to surround them with his presence and to accomplish his will back home. Their phone rang as I ended my prayer. The call was from the president's office of his country announcing that the government was in control and that those responsible for the coup attempt had been incarcerated. The ambassador's demeanor changed dramatically. He was so happy he walked with me all the way down the long outside stairway to the sidewalk, holding open the door to my car while I got in.

Who, I wondered, engineered the time of my visit and that phone call?

Six years later, the ambassador told me, "Ron, I am being recalled soon. When I return, I want to be a consultant to SIL to help with their relations between the church and our government. Please set up an itinerary for me to visit all of your training centers in the United States so I can familiarize myself with all that SIL is doing to help our people." (In his country, 280 languages are spoken.) I did set up a travel itinerary for him, and he visited our centers. Since returning to his home country, he has remained a friend and an in-country advocate for SIL.

BAWLING LIKE A BABY
WHEN HE SAID AMEN

On one of my last visits with Ambassador P., I confided in him about a family member over whom Ruth and I were heartbroken. At that moment, his secretary entered and told him that a prince from the Middle East was waiting to see him.

Expecting that he would ask me to leave in order to meet with the prince, I was surprised when instead, he said, "Let the prince wait." Ambassador P put his arm over my shoulders and prayed, asking for God's comfort and peace for Ruth and me. When he said amen, I was bawling like a baby. I thanked him and left. I don't know what the prince thought when I walked past him in tears, but in the years since then, God has answered that prayer and more for our family member.

YOUR INSTITUTE HAS NOT BEEN WITHOUT CONTROVERSY!

In April 1984 an ambassador from a South American country to Washington accepted a proposal to co-host a dinner with SIL. It featured the premiere viewing of the new film *Between Two Worlds* at the International Club in Washington. Invitations were sent on embassy letterhead over the ambassador's name to diplomats of other countries hosting SIL personnel. Diplomats from nine countries and their spouses attended the viewing.

The film tells the true story of a man of minority ethnicity who finds himself caught between his own Guahibo culture and the national Spanish culture. He opted to become literate first in his mother tongue and then in Spanish. At the end of the viewing, the ambassador stood up and thanked SIL for the film viewing. He then launched into colonial history and proposed the following: "The explorers came, but they were unsuccessful with the Indians. The conquistadors came, and they weren't successful. Nor have the church and its missionaries been successful in civilizing the Indians. But maybe language is the key."

Facing me, he said, "Your institute has not been without controversy. But I like that. When controversy occurs, something important is happening." On hearing this last statement, as far as I was concerned, the evening was a success. The dinner guests applauded.

Though explorers and missionaries were unsuccessful in "civilizing" the Indians, the lyrics of the first verse of this South American country's national anthem elaborate their legacy: "The fearful night has ceased. Sublime liberty shines forth the dawning of its invincible light. All of mankind, moaning in chains, understands the words of the one who died on the cross."

Is there any other nation with national anthem lyrics that reference Jesus Christ's death on the cross?

54

YES, LET'S DO IT

In 1990 I proposed an idea to Cameroon's ambassador: to cohost a reception in his embassy to celebrate SIL's twenty-five years in Africa. He said, "Yes, let's do it."

In preparation, we placed in the large embassy reception room a computer programmed with Cameroon language data and a printer. That evening during the reception, SIL interns Steve and Barbie Jacobsen would print out Cameroon language data on request. A number of visiting diplomats from other countries asked for printouts of language data from their particular country, but the computer was programmed only with Cameroon language data.*

The next morning Steve and I returned to the embassy to collect the computer and printer. We were surprised to see a number of the embassy staff—some standing, some sitting quietly reading the lists of languages spoken in Cameroon, which had been printed, read the previous evening, and then discarded. Most had no idea there were so many languages—271 known of at that time. I had no idea how important this information would be to them.

*SIL's *Ethnologue: Languages of the World* is a comprehensive reference work cataloging all of the world's known living languages. See www.ethnologue.com.

WISE COUNSEL

In 1988 SIL colleagues Dave Farah, Don Johnson, and I made a courtesy call on a newly arrived Latin American ambassador to Washington, D.C.

I posed the question, "What must SIL do to stay out of trouble in your country?"

His response was immediate: "You must, you must, you must"—his hand pounded the desk with each iteration—"keep all political leaders informed. Then, indirectly, you will have their support."

56

THE BEST ADVICE IN A LONG TIME

On a 1991 trip, when Ruth and I visited six African countries, we stopped in Cameroon to introduce the SIL director, Bob Creson, to Cameroon's former ambassador to the United States. Over dinner at Les Boukarous, an outdoor restaurant in Yaoundé, I told the former ambassador what the Latin American ambassador had told SIL in Washington—that we need to always keep all political leaders informed—and asked the former ambassador what he thought. He waxed eloquently in French for thirty minutes before concluding, "Yes. I agree with the ambassador from Latin America. You must keep all political leaders informed of your activities. Indirectly you will have their support." As Bob and I walked back to rejoin our wives after escorting the former ambassador to his car, Bob said, "That's the best advice I've had in a long time!"

PARTING STATEMENTS

In the fall of 1990, we helped celebrate the opening of the Museum of the Alphabet in Waxhaw, North Carolina. Our JAARS colleagues provided a DC-3 aircraft to fly diplomats and their wives from Washington, DC, to Waxhaw. Nine diplomats and their wives and visiting linguists from Cameroon and India joined us; Ruth and I accompanied them on the plane. One of the couples was from a Latin American country. I had not realized that he was also acting president of his country's senate. Speaking briefly to our JAARS colleagues, he said he had been responsible for introducing legislation that enabled the Indians of his country to pursue self-development. He told SIL's Adelmo Ruiz, "Get in touch with me if I can be of help."

Are not those kinds of parting statements to be taken seriously?

HERE'S OUR NUMBER AT HOME

A few months later, that embassy unexpectedly found itself as host to thirty orphans from its country visiting Washington, D.C. Somewhat in distress, embassy officials phoned the SIL office to ask if we could be of help in showing the orphans around the US capital.

At the time, SIL's Adelmo and Edelmira Ruiz of that country worked with me in the DC office. They responded to the embassy's urgent request for help by renting two vans and with their own two teenagers showed the orphans around America's capital city for a whole week. Obviously Adelmo and his family had done a huge favor for our friends in that embassy.

Not long after, we received another call from the SIL office in that country asking for help. Airplane parts had been sitting in customs for six months and were very much needed. This request came shortly after the Ruiz family had helped host the thirty orphans' Washington, DC, tour.

Adelmo said to me, "He [the ambassador] owes me one!" and phoned the embassy, asking to talk with him. The embassy secretary told Adelmo, "He is not here. Call his home." Adelmo phoned the residence, and the ambassador's wife said, "He is not here; he's at our home in the capital city, and here is our number. Call him. He will want to help you." Adelmo phoned the ambassador at his home number. That same day the aircraft parts were released from customs.

WE LAUGHED

In the late 1980s, while in New York, I was walking by Uganda's UN mission and decided to stop in and call on their representative to the United Nations—without an appointment.

After giving my card to the receptionist, he looked up, surprised, saying, "Oh!" He broke into a big grin. "*You* are Ron Gluck!" And then he explained his surprise. Before arriving in New York he had worked in Uganda's Ministry of External Affairs in Kampala and had been responsible for filing reports from their ambassador for each meeting, including ones with Ron Gluck of SIL.

Then I laughed and said, "Well, guess what! I've also been sending reports to our Dallas, Texas, headquarters of *my* meetings with your ambassadors."

We both laughed. What an encouragement and pleasure that I would be privileged to meet someone fresh from Uganda who already knew my name! His boss was not in the office, so he could not receive me.

Now, years later, I am reminded again just who does arrange such coincidences.

WE WANT TO RECIPROCATE

Our friends, the cultural attaché of an Asian country and his wife, were unable to accept SIL's invitation to Waxhaw, North Carolina, for the Alphabet Museum opening celebration but did ask if we would accompany them to the museum several weeks later. Ruth and I accepted their invitation, and on November 18, 1991, at 10 a.m., they came to our home in a chauffeur-driven four-door Mercury Marquis to begin the nine-hour drive south. We got in and had gone less than a mile when the cultural attaché, sitting in front, held up a yellow plastic Kodak bag, explaining that it was filled with audio cassette tapes of well-known arias and semi-classical American music themes. He said he had learned the music in high school and wanted to know if I would sing along with him as we traveled. Of course I agreed. He inserted cassette after cassette into the car cassette player and he and I sang Negro spirituals, gospel songs, popular tunes, etc. Four hours later we stopped for lunch near Raleigh, and I was much relieved, because my throat had gotten hoarse.

After lunch, we resumed traveling, and as the sun was setting, I heard the attaché talking with our young chauffeur. Then the attaché turned to me, asking if I would please drive because the chauffeur's night vision was not good. Of course I agreed, driving the last eighty miles. It was dark when we arrived at the JAARS center, our destination, where Dick and Kay Pittman had dinner waiting for us.

Our friends were much taken by the hospitality extended to them at the center and the simple lifestyles and commitment of the people they met. Of particular interest to them was funding of equipment, programs, and personal salaries.

They met with SIL linguists, who explained and answered queries about intricate language writing systems. A computer speech analyzer built by Rich Kelso intrigued them as they saw the audio waves of their voices reflected on a cathode-ray tube. A tour of the Museum of the Alphabet, the computer department, and the aviation facilities and a short helicopter ride provided scope to SIL's professional capability. The JAARS staff had planned marvelously for this visit. Our guests were impressed with the expertise of the people they met, who amazed them all the more by their "spirit of volunteerism," as our guests described it.

Before we departed, our guests were honored at the center staff meeting. The attaché used the occasion to express briefly his appreciation in English for their hospitality and ended his comments citing a verse from the New Testament: "By love, serve one another." It is the verse engraved on Cameron Townsend's* tombstone adjacent to the Museum of the Alphabet at the JAARS Center.

Again they asked me to drive the last eighty miles of our return trip. Ruth joined me up front, and the chauffeur sat in back with the attaché and his wife. For the last hour and a half they talked animatedly, I assumed of their experience in Waxhaw. Just before arriving at our home, the chauffeur leaned forward and said, "Mr. Gluck, would you please bring some SIL brochures to the embassy tomorrow? My boss wants to introduce your organization to our country's educational authorities." I could barely contain my excitement. Further, in response to the hospitality extended to them, they told me they wanted to invite eighty JAARS staff from Waxhaw, NC for dinner at the embassy in Washington, D.C.

*Cameron Townsend was not only the cofounder of SIL and WBT, but also the founder of JAARS.

61

YOU NEED HELP!

Following up that invitation, a date was set for dinner at the embassy in early 1992. A DC-3 planeload of twenty-eight passengers from the JAARS Center, along with fifteen local friends, SIL office staff, and SIL's Dr. Lon and Louise Diehl, who had been living in that nation for the past several years, were all guests of the embassy that evening. We were given a tour of the chancery with its colorful wall tapestries and ornate décor. A complete dinner of authentic Asian food was served by the embassy chefs, followed by two short movies.

Our host, the cultural attaché, then stood and spoke in English to his guests for perhaps ten minutes. After speaking, he said the evening was over and that we should leave. However, I managed to get his attention to tell him that SIL's Dr. Lon Diehl wished to respond. Our host stood aside and gestured for Lon to talk, which Lon did, in the national language.

As he began speaking, the kitchen staff poked their heads into the room to listen to this American speaking in their mother tongue. Lon's talk was short, and I do not know what he said.

Lon later told me, however, an Asian woman who was in the States temporarily came alongside him, quietly telling him, "You need help. Here is my husband's card. He works in the state commission. Call him. He will help you."

Lon had been trying for years to talk with an authority in that particular commission, but to no avail. None of us knew this woman, let alone that she would be in Washington at this reception.

Was her presence just another coincidence—or had it been arranged from above?

62

BUT THESE LANGUAGES ARE SPOKEN NEXT DOOR!

In fall of 1983, I called on a West African ambassador to Washington simply to inform him about SIL. He was a short, imposing figure, wearing thick eyeglasses with dark frames. At that time, his government had recently adopted a Marxist philosophy, and SIL had not signed an agreement with any national institution in the country but hoped to do so. That became the reason for follow-up visits.

I pulled some sample primers from my briefcase and handed them to him, briefly explaining that they were in the mother tongues of a neighboring country. He paged through several and then said, in French, "But these languages are spoken next door. Why aren't you working on languages of my country?" I explained that we would like to but did not know whom in the government to contact. He responded, saying his brother was the head linguist at the national university and that he would get in touch with him.

True to his word, within a couple of days, I received a copy of the letter to his brother, typed in French using Marxist jargon.

It began, "Cher Comrade," and talked briefly of SIL with instructions to contact SIL headquarters. The letter ended with this salutation over his name: *"La lutte continue!"* ("The battle continues!"). The following year, an accord was signed between the country's national university and SIL.

Was his brother's university position another coincidence—or part of a much larger plan?

63

HEY, GLUCK, IT'S ME!

Fast-forward to 1996, when, while in New York City calling on country representatives to the United Nations, my new boss Alan MacDonald and I made a cold call at the UN mission of the same country as in the previous segment.

It was a simple townhouse in Manhattan. I told the receptionist we would like to meet with the ambassador. As an embassy "gatekeeper," the young receptionist was a good one in that he would not allow us to see anyone in the embassy without learning more about us. Alan and I were seated uncomfortably in a too-small area. After some twenty minutes, it seemed we were getting nowhere. I felt frustrated and was about to stand up to leave when a voice behind me yelled, "Hey, Gluck, it's me! What are you doing here?"

It took a few moments for me to recognize the former ambassador to Washington. He was not wearing glasses, and I'd never seen him without them. I got up and shared a warm hug. I introduced Alan to him. Briefly, I told him the purpose of our visit, and then I asked what he was doing in New York.

He expressed appreciation for my attempt to call on him when Ruth and I passed through his country's capital in 1991.

"Oh," he began, "our foreign minister has named me inspector general of all our foreign missions. We have thirteen around the world, and I visit them all to make sure they are following our laws and regulations for diplomacy. Let's go upstairs and visit."

The receptionist was observing and listening to this verbal exchange. His attitude toward us had done a quick 180. Now, he was smiling and couldn't do enough to help get us upstairs and out of his space. I was careful to thank him. He really had done his job well, and in the years following, he welcomed me warmly whenever I visited.

Was making a cold call and unexpectedly meeting the former ambassador just coincidental—again?

64

THIS IS SEDFREY

In the summer of 1986, I received a phone call from Sedfrey. I didn't know Sedfrey and asked what he wanted. He gave me his full name, Sedfrey Ordonez, explaining that he was from the Philippines and visiting his daughter in DC, and then asked to come by for a visit.

Over a cup of tea, he informed me that he was a charter member of SIL's advisory committee in the Philippines, and whenever he traveled abroad, he always checked in with the local SIL personnel to see if he could be of help. And now, at President Cory Aquino's request, he was on his way to New York to assume the position of the Philippines permanent representative to the UN. I wished him well, informing him that I hoped to be in New York in the fall. He asked that we please stop in to see him in New York and said he would help us in any way he could.

Two years earlier, in 1984, heeding the advice of Ed Davis of our local advisory committee, we—the DC SIL staff—had begun making three-day trips to New York City each fall. The trips coincided with the reconvening of the UN General Assembly at which heads of states and prime ministers often attended.

Engaging with representatives of the same governments in New York that we met with in D.C. reinforced our mission of keeping government leaders informed of language related developments in their country. Cooperative agreements with their national institutions make it somewhat easy to obtain appointments with these diplomats.

Initially the Christian Embassy—part of Campus Crusade—in NYC kindly made space available in their offices from which we could confirm an appointment itinerary and operate out of while in NYC. Its location was also convenient, being a one-block walk to the UN Secretariat. Two years later, the Christian Embassy moved its office to a church in mid-Manhattan. That move reinforced our need for other office digs during our brief stays in New York.

In August 1986 I contacted Sedfrey, explaining our need for a small space from which to base activities while in New York. He wasn't sure extra space in their UN mission was available but said to come there anyway. Our team of five went from the Amtrak train station straight to the Philippines UN mission. Sedfrey welcomed us and escorted us to the sixth floor—an apartment completely equipped for their visiting VIPs.

Josefina, Sedfrey's wife, stayed in the apartment that whole first day, serving us cake she had baked with freshly made coffee.

When other UN missions returned phone calls about appointments we had requested, they were greeted by a Filipino voice with "Philippines mission" instead of "Christian Embassy."

In my mind's eye, I could see "Uncle Cam" Townsend, the late cofounder of SIL, smiling. It was a classic example of host government-SIL cooperation that he himself modeled and encouraged.

65

TODAY, I AM REMOVING MY MASK

In July 1986 we held an outdoor picnic in Alexandria, Virginia, in order to welcome President Aquino's newly appointed ambassador, Manny Palaez of the Philippines, to Washington.

He told the guests, who included diplomats from nine other countries and local friends, a bit of his life story, describing himself as a typical politician. He had been elected as a senator to the Congress of the Philippines. Then President Marcos attempted to have him ambushed late one night because the political positions of the then senator conflicted with those of the president.

The senator's chauffeur was killed outright, and the senator himself was rushed to hospital with five bullets lodged near his heart. While in the hospital and near death, his sister read to him from the Psalms, and he clung to the words "I will praise your name while I have my being" (Psalm 104:33 American Standard Version).

In 1986, when Cory Aquino was elected president of the Philippines, she sent Senator Pelaez to Washington as her ambassador. He continued, "I was told by friends in Manila that I'm coming to Washington as a missionary disguised as an ambassador. But today, I am removing my mask."

He also told the assembled guests that he had invited God into his life and had found a new purpose in living. Then he described the circumstances leading to the downfall of President Marcos and the election of Cory Aquino, whose husband had also been ambushed and killed.

On numerous occasions after that picnic, I visited Ambassador Pelaez, once asking for the intervention and help of his government when SIL's Eunice Dimont was kidnapped by guerillas in the Southern Philippines. Ambassador Pelaez agreed to convey SIL's request that guns not be used in the pursuit to free Eunice Dimont. She was released a week later.

66

YOU'RE NOT HERE ABOUT OUR DEFENSE POSTURE?

I had met the more recent Philippines ambassador, Ambassador R., just once previously. My purpose in calling on him this time was to see if he would host an evening in which we could present to the embassy the gift of a rather large painting of a Philippines village teacher and pupil setting by SIL artist Hyatt Moore.

On entering his office, Ambassador R. welcomed me, telling me that he thought his government had complied with all of our requests and wondered if there was something more that we wanted. I wasn't quite sure what he was referring to and asked if he could elaborate. It then became evident he thought I was with the US Department of State and had come to talk about the Philippines' defense posture.

The focus of conversation quickly changed to the purpose of why I was there. He agreed eagerly to host a dinner reception.

On that reception evening, Greg Dekker, SIL director of the Philippines, was in DC to make the presentation of the painting to the ambassador. But Greg had gotten lost, arrived late, and wasn't even wearing a tie or jacket for the function. I quickly herded him into the men's room, removed my own jacket, shirt, and tie, and gave them to him to change into. I then put on his sport shirt, and the event went smoothly.

One of the consular staff ladies, during the traditional dancing, grabbed my arm and pulled me into the center to dance. I'm not a very graceful guy but did my best. Some SIL colleagues standing against the wall burst out laughing at me, but it was a fun evening.

On my next visit to the embassy I noticed the painting had been mounted on the wall in plain view of everyone entering the embassy through the front main entrance.

WHY DO YOU KEEP NO OTHER WOMEN?

In 1995, the Indonesian embassy press information officer and his wife came to our home for dinner, bringing along their fourteen-year-old daughter.

We were all seated at the table and eating, when out of the blue, his wife, seated next to me, faced me and asked, "Mr. Gluck, why do you keep no other women?" I responded that it was because of a promise I had made before God when Ruth and I exchanged wedding vows in 1962 to be faithful to one another. And besides, I said, "I love her and her only." She nodded in understanding. So I then posed her question to her husband. And he answered, "It is for the same reasons you gave."

Ruth and I later agreed his wife had probably asked the question for the benefit of their daughter, believing, perhaps, that our response would be trustworthy.

OF COURSE. THAT'S WHY
WE MARRY THEM!

In August 1986, the Indonesian embassy invited its "friends" to their National Day reception. (America's national day is the Fourth of July.) My invitation was for 6:30 to 8:00 p.m. on a warm, humid August Friday at the embassy.

Instead, I went home at five o'clock, and Ruth asked, "Why aren't you going to the reception?"

I said, "It's hot, and it's a typical summer weekend of rush-hour traffic downtown."

"You need to go," she said. "It's your job."

Reluctantly, I agreed, putting my tie back on and grabbing a dark-blue jacket, and headed back downtown. I parked at the first spot that I came to within walking distance, put my jacket over my arm, and began walking to the embassy.

At the corner of Massachusetts and North Twenty-First Street NW, a half block ahead, I saw guests standing in a line that extended onto the sidewalk, waiting to enter the embassy, and took my place at the end of it. On reaching the first set of steps, my friend Robi, the consular officer, greeted me.

"Ah, Mr. Gluck, how are you?" We exchanged greetings. "I need to see your invitation." After showing it to him, he said, "You need to enter that door." I thanked him and before long found myself inside the front entrance. The military attaché took my name and then passed it on to the ambassador standing next to him.

I thanked the ambassador for my invitation, saying, "You know, I think we've met somewhere." He responded with a smile, "Yes, I think we have, but I don't remember where!" He then introduced me to his wife, who introduced me to other staff until, at the end of the receiving line, a friend, the educational attaché, took my arm and escorted me to the food table. There, the attaché's wife promptly got a plate, filled it with samples of Indonesian cuisine, and handed it to me.

Then the press officer, who had been to our home, replaced the attaché, took my arm, and had his wife retrieve a delicious fruit drink for me. We stood and chatted briefly. The political situation in the Middle East was heating up at that time, and I made a mental note that he had introduced me to an Iraqi printer who printed embassy publications. I saw my new friend there also, the ambassador from Papua New Guinea, and was able to introduce them to each other. It seemed like only a few minutes had elapsed, but when I glanced at my watch, it was almost eight o'clock.

Traditional dancing then began near the front entrance of the embassy. Slowly I made my way to the front door to exit, when the attaché came alongside again. I commented to him on the beauty of their women dancers.

He said, "Of course. That's why we marry them!" We both laughed. I told him how much I had enjoyed the evening and thanked him for his help and advice over the years as educational attaché. We bid each other a good evening and I left.

It was cooler outside, and Robi was still at the top of the first set of stairs, greeting late guests. I couldn't see him, because my eyes had not adjusted to the outside darkness, but he saw me.

"Ah, Mr. Gluck, how was it?"

"Wonderful," I replied.

Then he asked, "How come you don't come by for visas anymore?"

I answered, "You know, Robi, the requirements to enter your country have changed, and our people can now obtain their visas upon arrival in Jakarta."

He said, "Yes, that's right. Come by anyway. I'll see you next time." We shook hands, and I began walking down the sidewalk in the direction of my parked car.

Suddenly, I was overcome with emotion as I thought about the evening and had to stop walking. I leaned against a tree nearby, thinking particularly of the friends that had stayed by my side all evening. Of course that was part of their job, making guests feel welcome. But their camaraderie and conversations with me were deeper than light chatter.

Weren't relationships a gift that God had superintended, enabling the enjoyable friendship of officials of governments hosting SIL, and resulting collaboration—be it with visas or language policy—facilitating written development of the nation's mother tongues?

69

BUT YOU HAVE ELECTRICITY!

In December 1986, I took some passports with visa applications to a Central African embassy to leave with the consular officer. The front door was ajar as I entered the building. Inside, there was no heat, nor was there a receptionist. But the door to the consular office was closed, so I knocked, and a familiar voice invited me in. The room was being warmed by an electric heater, and Mr. Omer was alone, seated at a desk behind the counter, reading from the Bible.

I asked him what he was reading.

Smiling, he said, "Nehemiah." Still smiling, he added, "This book will change your life."

I nodded in agreement and asked, "What's going on? No heat!"

In French, he explained, "Yes, they've cut off the gas, and they've cut off the water."

I pointed to a light shining overhead and to the electric heater, saying, "But you have electricity."

He responded, "Ah, yes, they'll cut that off too. The embassy has received no money from our government. We've not been paid for five and a half months. Soon it will be six."

"How are you paying for food?"

"Local store proprietors know what's going on. They give us credit.

"The visas will be ready in two weeks," he said. I thanked him, bid him good-bye and left.

Back at the SIL office, I phoned the Congo state department desk officer, asking if he couldn't be of help. He responded, "We know about these cases, but if we provide them with funding, it removes pressure on their government to take care of its own personnel."

Two weeks later, I returned, stopping en route to buy three chickens at the local grocery store, and hid them from the consul's view on entering. The building was still cold. We exchanged greetings, and with a smile, he handed me the passports I'd come for.

With the passports in hand, I gave the chickens to Mr. Omer and told him to pass them around as Christmas gifts to other embassy staff. Of course he was very appreciative. From then on, he called me *"mon Père,"* French for "my Father," a title given to Catholic priests.

What quality of character impels someone to come to work faithfully for the government, showing up even when wages are not being paid month after month? Was there a hidden fear of retribution? Or did he believe it was simply the right thing to do?

In hindsight I should have prayed with him and for leaders of his government before leaving.

CAN YOU HELP US DISPOSE OF THESE MIGS?

The ambassador of a country in southern Africa phoned to ask for my help in the late 1980s. He knew I had been a pilot. The country's previous government had embraced a communist philosophy, and, as wards of the former Soviet Union, his government had been recipients of aging MIG-13 Russian fighter jets that were no longer flyable due to lack of spare parts.

The ambassador asked, "Can you help us"—meaning his government—"dispose of these MIGs and sell them?"

I wasn't sure, but I promised to do what I could. Fellow JAARS pilot Bob Griffin, at my request, sent me a copy of an aviation weekly publication, *Trade-a-Plane*. As the name implies, it contained ads from plane enthusiasts wanting to buy and sell airplanes. In particular, there was a high demand for older warplanes that buyers would refurbish. I gave the journal to the ambassador, pointing out the ads to him. He was pleased and thanked me.

YOU MEAN AN ILS—AN
INSTRUMENT LANDING SYSTEM?

Not long after, that ambassador again phoned, asking me to come see him. Could I help his government obtain airport equipment required for planes to land in bad weather?

"Do you mean an Instrument Landing Systems, an ILS?" I asked.

He shrugged his shoulders, saying, "If that's what it is."

Again I said, "I'm not sure I can be of help, but I will see what I can find out."

This was before the days of Google. But a short time later, I was able to provide him with the names and telephone numbers of American manufacturers of ILS systems that his government could contact.

The question could be posed, "What does this and helping with his previous request have to do with language development and Bible translation?"

One could answer, "Nothing"—or one could answer, "Everything." This man is a friend of SIL. He was recalled to assume the position of deputy minister of foreign affairs. At the time of writing this, SIL personnel have no problem obtaining visas to enter his country.

The deputy minister is knowledgeable of and appreciates SIL's language activities in his country.

72

MOI, JE PRÉFÈRE LA TÊTE!

In October 1983, two weeks after paying a courtesy call on the newly arrived ambassador from a small West African country to Washington, I received a call from him. He informed me that in two weeks' time, the country's head of state would be arriving in Washington on a state visit to meet with President Reagan. Further, the ambassador wanted us to give a report to his president of SIL's activities in his country. I promised him that we would give a report.

In the meantime, I learned that his president was an avid hunter and began wondering what we could give him as a gift. The SIL director of that country, Paul Meier, was then in the United States attending board meetings. I contacted Paul and told him of this coming event, which I viewed as a wonderful opportunity.

Paul responded in his Swiss-German English, "Ron, I can't do it. This man's political philosophy does not encourage what we are doing. I can't come. And besides, I have no good clothes for such a visit, nor money to cover travel to Washington."

I suggested to Paul that he pray about it.

He called back within a few hours, telling me that several other SIL branch directors had gotten together, encouraged him to come, and had also agreed to pay his round-trip fare to Washington.

After he arrived in Washington, someone anonymously bought Paul a new suit of clothes. The night before calling on the head of state, my wife, Ruth, hemmed the pants of Paul's new suit, and the next morning, Dave Witmer and I accompanied Paul to the hotel for our appointment with the head of state.

I took the initiative to welcome the president to DC and told him that we would like to give him, as a gift, either the horns or the skin of an American wild animal. Which would he prefer?

There was a pause, and in French, he answered, *"Moi, je préfère la tête!"*—in English: "I prefer the head!"

Paul then took the initiative of reading the first ten verses of First John in French to the president and explained SIL's motivation and language activities. The president seemed pleased with our visit. We thanked him for the interview and excused ourselves. In the hallway outside his door the TV media crew that had accompanied the president surrounded us, posing questions, asking primarily what had been discussed. Paul used the country's national television to describe SIL's language activities in the country. Paul never saw the news clip of his interview, but later wrote to us that upon returning, missionaries told him, "You have done a wonderful thing for all of us!"

73

PASSING THE BUCK

As we left the hotel after meeting with the president, Paul was excited. His attitude had markedly changed. He exclaimed, "Ron, we've got to get a gift worthy of the president—a moose head!"

I responded, "Paul, that's huge! Who's going to pay for it, plus the shipping?"

His response: "The Lord will provide!"

Several days later, SIL's North America branch director phoned to tell me that his branch was sending us the mounted head of a ten-point buck in a crate and that it would be arriving by Trailways Bus.

Dave Witmer and I retrieved it at the Trailways/Greyhound bus station in DC. The crate barely fit into the back of my Chevy Citation, but we managed to transport it to my house in Arlington, Virginia. The crate had become loose and wobbly in transit, so we dismantled it, made it smaller and stronger, and then delivered it to the embassy with the stuffed deer head inside.

The ambassador looked at it, asking what kind of animal it was. I explained it was a like a cerf, which is prevalent in Africa, and that we called it a deer. He asked who killed it. I told him we didn't know.

He thanked us and told us to put the top on. He would have it shipped to the president. This shipment by the embassy was a wonderful provision. We think of it as . . . the passing of the buck.

74

LANGUAGE DISPUTE SETTLED

In a letter to Paul Meier, I said that the buck head was being shipped by the embassy and that separately we would send him a plaque that would mark the occasion of the president's visit to Washington. He could then use a presentation of the plaque as a reason to obtain a follow-up appointment and then make a request of the president that could easily be granted.

Americans Tom and Esther Marmor had been working in the Kabiye communities with and through the Kabiye Language Committee. Kabiye was the mother tongue of the president. The Marmors had studied Kabiye, developed an alphabet, and analyzed the grammar system; they had begun literacy classes to teach Kabiye people how to read the language they spoke. The Marmors had also begun the translation of a Kabiye New Testament.

Paul was granted an appointment and delivered the plaque to the head of state, who then told Paul that it was right for him to follow up the Washington visit. During this second visit, Paul sought the president's advice on a language question. The president thought for a moment and then made a decision, answering the question, which according to Paul ended an ongoing, longtime disagreement among foreign missionaries in the country. However, he never told us what the palaver was about.

PRESIDENT HELPED DISTRIBUTE MARK

On one occasion, Tom Marmor went to the president's village specifically to meet him there and present copies of the newly translated book of Mark in Kabiye. As Tom explained, it was important to present such materials to him before distributing them.

The president then handed out copies of Mark to several government ministers who had accompanied him to the village.

Was it simply a coincidence that several government ministers had accompanied the president and were in his village that day?

WE WANT TO COME HOME!

One spring, in the late 1980s, an ambassador from West Africa phoned, requesting that I come see him.

I went to his office, and he told me that he had two nieces visiting from France over the summer and wanted to know if I had any ideas of ways to entertain them.

This was a new challenge; I wasn't sure how to help.

But back at my office, I called Wycliffe's office in Lancaster, Pennsylvania, to ask for their ideas, and a few days later they called back with the names of two families near Lancaster who had each agreed to host one of the girls. The ambassador was delighted!

His wife accompanied me as I drove the two nieces to Lancaster. They were each introduced to their host families. Then she and I returned to DC.

On the first night, both nieces called their uncle, in tears, wanting to "come home." They didn't like their circumstances in Lancaster. But he insisted they stay.

Two weeks later, the ambassador himself traveled with me as we returned to Lancaster to pick up the two teenagers. From the time they climbed into the backseat of the car, they talked nonstop, excitedly, giggling and laughing.

The ambassador, seated beside me up front, was listening, smiling, and on occasion was also giggling. Later I learned that one of the young girls had attended Young Life meetings with the daughter of her host family and had invited Christ into her life.

77

YOUR LEADERS PRAY

The US Congress each year issues invitations to all foreign ambassadors—that is, those posted to the UN, the OAS and to Washington, DC—to the National Prayer Breakfast. The ambassador of the same West African country to the UN, a friend, attended one year.

Some months later, I was in New York City, and we lunched together. While still at the table, after we had eaten, he moved his head close to mine and said in a very low voice, "I think I know why the United States is so blessed. Your leaders pray together."

I agreed.

In retrospect this annual event was and continues to be a tremendous blessing to our nation and to the world. It is a forum for political, social and business elite to assemble and build relationships.

At the 1988 National Prayer Breakfast Africa dinner at the Washington Hilton Hotel, the head of state of a neighboring country spoke at length about the history of his nation's involvement in the slave trade. Speaking specifically to black Americans at the dinner, he said something I had never heard previously.

He said, "There were buyers and there were sellers. Yes, the Europeans and the West were the buyers. But it was our own ancestral chiefs who were the sellers—selling their own people into slavery."

He then got down on his knees on the podium and said, "On behalf of our mutual ancestral chiefs, I beg your forgiveness."

Some twenty-four months before that dinner, this head of state had invited Christ into his life.

SIL IS ALWAYS WELCOME AT MY DOOR

In 1996, Ruth and I returned to Africa and visited six countries for the purpose of introducing local SIL administrators to diplomats who had returned home—some to retire, and some who had been given increased government responsibility.

One gentleman we called on in West Africa was Victor, that country's former ambassador to the United Nations. He had visited the JAARS center in Waxhaw, North Carolina, and seen the tools of technology at the disposal of SIL's linguists to use in support of the development of unwritten languages and translation of the Scriptures.

When I introduced the SIL director of that country to Victor, Victor said, "When I visited your technical center in Waxhaw, North Carolina, I had just been named to preside over the Security Council of the United Nations. And in each home I visited in Waxhaw, the people prayed for me. SIL programs enable people in my country to make informed decisions. SIL is always welcome at my door."

YOUR PRAYER IS THE
BENEDICTION TO YOUR VISIT

In October 1987, my boss, Aaron Hoffman, accompanied me to New York on an appointment with another West African nation's ambassador to the UN. We were seated in the waiting room adjacent to the ambassador's office.

I could sense something akin to a crisis was bubbling. The ambassador was barking orders to staff, who were literally running in and out of his office.

Finally, he stuck his head into the waiting room and barked, "Come in." Aaron and I followed him into his office, where he motioned for us to sit on a couch. He explained that his government had decided to build a new embassy in Jerusalem, and now all the Arab nations were threatening to sever relations with his government. As he talked, the phone rang, and he answered it immediately. While he talked on the phone, I observed two long telex messages stretching across his desk all the way to the floor on each side of his desk.

Thirty minutes later, the ambassador hung up the phone, saying he had been talking with their ambassador to Cairo, who wanted advice. He had just been summoned to the Egyptian Foreign Ministry to explain the decision to build a new embassy in Jerusalem. Then he pointed to the two telexes across his desk, explaining they were instructions from his president on how to explain that decision to the Arab governments. It was obvious this was an awkward moment for this ambassador to receive us.

I asked him if he was Muslim or Christian. Both, he answered. Would he mind if I offered a prayer for wisdom?

"Please do."

In French, I prayed a prayer for wisdom, the kind of prayer I would have wanted prayed for me if I were in his shoes, in the strong name of Jesus, and said, "Amen."

He thanked me, adding, "Your prayer is the benediction to your visit."

Twelve months later, Steve Jacobson and I returned to call on him and were ushered to the Delegates' Lounge in the UN Secretariat and told to wait. The lounge area itself was empty except for two Secret Service men who came over and searched our handbags.

All of a sudden, I recognized Israel's Prime Minister Shamir Perez entering the lounge. He walked over to shake our hands and then walked to another corner and conferred with his aides.

An aide of the ambassador with whom we had an appointment then arrived and led us to the bar, where his boss was waiting. The ambassador was smiling and greeted us, pointing to two stools next to him and asking what we'd like to drink. "Coca-Cola?"

"Okay," I replied.

He barked, pleasantly, "Bartender, three Coca-Colas, please."

Then he asked, "Let me see what you have there." Steve and I had brought along reading primers in languages SIL linguists in the ambassador's country were helping to develop into written form. I asked if he really wanted to study them there at the bar.

"Yes, lay them out. I want to see them."

So I opened several small primer booklets, laying them on the bar. He had paged through them for several minutes, nodding in approval over each, when a loud buzzer sounded.

"Oh," he said, "that means Prime Minister Shamir is about to speak to the General Assembly, and I need to go in and show our government's support for Israel. Have you ever been to the General Assembly Hall?"

I shook my head no.

"Well, follow me." He led us to the big UN General Assembly hall frequently seen on television.

He pointed to his seat and waved good-bye, saying he'd see us next year, and then walked to his desk, his left arm wrapped around the stack of reading primers he had been given.

The ambassador could not have been friendlier. Was it because of the prayer for wisdom offered on his behalf twelve months earlier?

80

PEOPLE STUDYING OUR LANGUAGES BACK HOME!

While standing, watching and listening to Israel's Prime Minister greet the General Assembly, I heard someone speaking French behind me, saying, "This is the one I was telling you about. They have people studying our languages back home."

I turned around and was greeted by the ambassador from another Francophone country, who then introduced me to his boss, the minister of foreign affairs (a position that is the equivalent of the American secretary of state).

That minister then asked me what we were doing with the languages of his country. I explained briefly that we were studying some of them and helping to put them into writing.

"Will you have time to meet in the afternoon?" he asked.

I answered, "No, we'll be returning to Washington this afternoon."

"I'll be in Washington this weekend," he said. "Maybe we can meet there?"

I agreed, and so on Sunday, I went to the residence of his government's ambassador in Washington and met with the foreign minister, giving him a list of the languages I had researched that SIL personnel were studying in his country.

He looked at the list, saying, "But these are all small languages! Why don't you work in the larger languages?"

I told him I wasn't sure, but that it was possible that if the languages spoken by smaller ethnicities were not written and recorded, they might disappear over time.

"Yes, that might be true," he commented.

I also told him it was an opportunity to help translate the Scriptures of the Bible into those smaller languages. He thanked me, and we parted company. Question: Was where I was standing at end of the previous story segment that resulted in meeting with this foreign minister simply -- coincidence?

81

COLLEY

Colley became a friend. I saw him almost every weekday afternoon at the Farragut West subway station in Washington, DC, on the corner of I and Eighteenth Streets NW. He would stand at ground level next to the down escalator, leaning on his long white cane, greeting people heading home with a "God bless you" and a smile. He was a tall, thin, blind young man and always wore dark glasses and a cap.

One afternoon I heard him shouting, "Roses! Three for four dollars or six for five!"

I approached and said, "Colley, this is Ron. I don't see any roses you're selling. Where are they?"

"Hey, Ron," he greeted me. "My friend Mike is selling them over there on the sidewalk." He pointed, and I saw someone who I assumed was Mike and several large white buckets of water containing many, many different colored long-stemmed roses.

Colley continued, "Mike's my friend, and we help each other when we can."

One afternoon, I saw Colley on the sidewalk corner of I and Nineteenth Streets NW, one block west of the station. He was calling out asking for help, but no one stopped. I greeted him, asking what he was doing on that corner. He said he was trying to get to I and Eighteenth but didn't know where he was, and no one would help him.

Placing my hands on his shoulders, I turned his body to face Eighteenth Street, one block away.

With that he started happily walking down the sidewalk toward Eighteenth Street NW and said, "Thanks a lot. See ya 'round, man."

That was around year 2003 or 2004 and was the last time I saw Colley.

Question: by standing next to the down escalator leading to the subway, was this good-natured, smiling man God's way, perhaps, of reminding commuters of the blessing of sight?

Lt. Gluck in F-86L Greater Pittsburgh Airport –
circa 1958, permission Air National Guard

Typical New Guinea highlands village
scene – circa 1966 photo by author

New Guinea Western Highlands villagers listening to
texts in mother tongue - circa 1966 photo by author

Author fueling Cessna 185 at Aiyura, New
Guinea circa 1965 – photo by Ruth Gluck

Woodwind instrumentalists at Kelobo New
Guinea – circa 1966 photo by Ruth Gluck

Moving – Buka Island, New Guinea- circa 1968 photo by author

Mother tongue writing class – Cameroon – circa1975 – photo by Ruth Gluck

SIL Cessna 206 1st landing opens Garoua Boulai new airstrip -- Cameroon circa 1975 -- photo by author

Language, Culture, Faith, Translation, and Life Morsels

A Mélange of Vignettes throughout Forty-Four Years That Encourage Us along the Way

82

MBAKA PYGMY CHIEF: "WE'VE BEEN WAITING A LONG TIME!"

Kath Higgins was British, Margreet Vogelaar was Dutch, and they partnered in 1979. My SIL colleague Dick Stewart and I accompanied them to the southeast corner of Cameroon, just north of Mouloundou, where they wished to locate and begin studying the Mbaka language. The Mbaka people are of small stature and, for want of a better term, are often called pygmies.

Utmost among Kath's concerns was housing. Where would they live? Would they need to build their own house? And how would they obtain potable water?

From Catholic Relief Service in Yaoundé we borrowed a Toyota four-wheel drive pickup, and along with Kath's new Russian Jeep—both vehicles heavily loaded with supplies—we drove for three days toward Moulundou, the Mbaka area. After introducing ourselves to local government officials in the nearest town, we continued on and stopped at a Mbaka village.

In French, I called out, asking for the chief. A man of short height came forward. The people accompanying him and surrounding us were also short in stature. Also, everyone seemed to have pointed teeth. (I later learned that as children approached their eleventh year, parents would file their children's teeth into points—a mark of beauty.)

Through the interpreter, I explained in French to the chief that (1) these women had come to live in your village and learn your talk; (2) they want to write down your talk (here I showed him a letter of authorization on Cameroon government letterhead authorizing study of the Mbaka language); and (3) they would also help turn God's talk into your talk.

As I talked to the chief, another Mbaka man loudly mimicked me and made threatening gestures. But the chief disregarded his angry brother and responded to me quickly. "We've been waiting a long time!" he said. The mocking ended.

"They will need your help," I told him. "You must provide housing for them. People must bring them food and teach them your talk."

As soon as what I said was interpreted to him, he turned around, barking orders to the people surrounding us. Like a stampede, they all ran at once to the largest house at one end of the village and began tossing out all the stuff that was inside. They also started repairing the roof. Then the personal effects and supplies of the two women were emptied from the borrowed Toyota and Kath's Jeep and carried into the little house.

As Dick and I drove away, I saw Kath out of the corner of my eye. She was teary-eyed but appeared to be writing phonetically to record the expressions and terms she was hearing in the Mbaka tongue. I also saw Margreet, six feet tall, down on all fours attempting to get through the low entrance of their new, low, small home. It was the best-constructed "house" in the village.

What had just occurred in less than thirty minutes was amazing! Kath and Margreet had been given a warm acceptance *and* housing among the Mbaka people.

Who arranged for this warm reception?

Was it also indicative of a deep hunger to know God?

If so, who creates such hunger?

"OH, GREAT CHIEF OF HEAVEN"—A SALT-YUI PRAYER

Around 1967, Barry Irwin's Salt-Yui language helper in PNG, before beginning the project of translating Matthew into the Salt-Yui tongue, asked to pray. Here is Barry's English translation of the prayer by his language helper:

Oh, Great Chief of heaven, you alone are the possessor of strength. You alone are the possessor of the being and remaining life. With you alone rest all foundation words. Therefore, we worship you and greet you now. We are not strong. We need your being and remaining life. We know nothing. Our ears are stopped, and we do not know the foundation words. But despite all this we have now come to work for you. Send your very spirit into the center of our beings so that he may put aside our stupidity and show us what we need to know. May he help the pink-skin and may he help us black-skinned men so that together we may be able to scratch and put the foundation words on the banana leaf [paper].

MARCHING WHITE LIGHTS

It happened one evening in 1967 in PNG at the conclusion of the weekly Bible Study for SIL employees who met in our home. After our guests had all left, I stepped outside the front door and looked up into the sky, bright with blinking stars. It seemed I was looking up into a colorful sanctuary—a remarkable, majestic temple of stars in the southern hemisphere. There was no mistaking the Southern Cross.

The star and moonlit vista facing south also revealed acres and acres of rolling hills covered with long kunai grass gently waving with the evening breeze in the Ukarumpa Valley.

But that night my eyes were also drawn toward the southwest to what seemed an endless stream of tiny white lights of equal intensity on a hill maybe a half mile distant. The lights, very evenly spaced, were all moving (walking?) in tandem. The front of that line was maybe a half mile away, and appeared headed in the direction of Ukarumpa Village, situated maybe a mile distant and beyond the end of the Aiyura airstrip. They would pass west of our house and the SIL center by maybe a thousand feet. Growing up I had heard stories of how Satan manifests himself in a variety of ways in areas of the world where people have no knowledge of Christ. I had not forgotten 2 Corinthians 11:14, which says, "Satan himself masquerades as an angel of light." (New International Version)

The scene was intriguing. I watched for several minutes as the tiny white lights kept moving in tandem, equidistantly spaced. Then I realized the front leading light had taken a new direction, leading all of the lights in a line straight to our home. Suddenly, I felt vulnerable and exposed and went back into the house, locked the front and back doors, and asked God in the strong name of Jesus to protect our home and family.

Were the white lights a manifestation of Satan, angry because people of Papua New Guinea were hearing and reading of Jesus and promises from God's Word for the first time ever?

The next morning was bright and sunny, but no one that I asked had seen that parade of tiny white lights the previous night.

IS PRAYER PRACTICAL?

It was the dry season in 1974. An epidemic of meningitis had broken out in a Bankim village one hour flying time north of Yaoundé, Cameroon. Since it spreads quickly through dust, the only hope of stopping the epidemic seemed to be rain. The principal at the mission school there called all the teachers together to pray for rain.

The next day it rained, and the epidemic ended—just a coincidence?

READING NSO

Christopher was the house steward of Karl and Winnie Grebe and had also become, on his own initiative, their main literacy promoter, managing book sales and more. The Grebes purchased an 80cc motorcycle for him to use so that on weekends and whenever he had spare time he could scoot around to different villages selling books of Lamnso folklore* and portions of Scripture, as well as interest people in learning to read their mother tongue.

One Sunday morning, at a church attended by Lamnso people, church leaders put Christopher on the spot, asking him to read passages in their language out loud from the Gospel of Mark that Karl and the Lamnso language team had translated. Apparently the people thought only a well-educated person like Karl could read their language. They had heard it was hard to read Lamnso. Now they were testing Christopher to see if one of their own who had only a minimal formal education had really learned to read their language.

He passed the test easily. The listeners were very, very excited to realize their language could be written and read. Several bought books, and a number of Lamnso people then asked to be taught how to read in their mother tongue. A new reading class was planned with Christopher as the teacher.

What a game changer—to realize your language can be written by creating its own alphabet and read just like French or English or any major language of wider communication!

*Recorded folklore stories are the primary source of language sounds studied and analyzed by linguists in determining significant sounds in order to create an alphabet, studying grammar, and writing the language.

87

WHERE DID I JUST SEE THIS?

In 1979, I went to Cameroon's immigration office in Yaoundé to obtain the residence permit renewals of an SIL married couple. The official indicated a chair for me to sit in and wait. It was a wooden chair with a webbed center, most of which was missing. Apprehensively I sat on the edge of it and looked around. The walls had long ago been painted a cream color but over time were covered with red dust. On the wall close beside me was an open receptacle box with exposed electrical wiring. The electric receptacle that had once been there was missing.

In my mind, I reasoned, *Yup—the government didn't provide or have budget for cleaning.*

A few moments later, the immigration officer motioned for me to come sit in a chair beside his desk. I greeted him and explained what I needed. He wanted more information about the couple, so I told him of the location where they were living and the language they were studying.

Watching his face closely, I perceived just the tiniest smile, barely noticeable. When I asked what his mother tongue was, it was the same language that Keith and Mary Beavon were studying and whose residence permits I was submitting for renewal.

No, he didn't know Keith and Mary, but he had heard of them. He told me to leave their documents and retrieve the renewals in a few days, which is how it worked out.

But who, I wondered, arranged this set of "coincidences"— that the guy granting the renewals would be a speaker of that tongue that the couple requesting them were also studying and helping put into written form?

A few months later, while in the United States for JAARS board meetings, I stopped in Baltimore, Maryland, at the DMV office to renew my Maryland driver's license. The secretary indicated a stuffed chair for me to sit in and wait. I sat in it, sinking all the way to the floor. Support strapping in the chair was long gone. The office walls beside the chair were painted green, but had been soiled by many dirty hands and fingers. Near the chair was an electric receptacle dangling loose from the wall, attached only by a lone wire.

To myself, I thought, *Yup—maintenance of government facilities is lacking, no doubt, because the budget was already stretched thin.*

Wait, I tried remembering, *where was I just in this scenario?*

Isn't development in this context relative, anyway?

88

WHY MUST YOU KNOW . . .?

Emmanuel Njock became a close friend. He had earned a doctorate in linguistics in Canada and was now the headmaster of a high school in Libamba, in Cameroon's South-Central Province. It was a boarding school started by American Presbyterian missionaries.

Like other Cameroonians I had met, when we'd see each other, he would ask me where I was coming from, what I was doing, and where I was going. I found these questions annoying. To me they seemed intrusive.

One day, when we met up unexpectedly in the SIL center, he asked them of me again.

I lashed out, "Emmanuel! Why do you ask me these questions when we meet—where I've been, what I'm doing, where I'm going? It's none of your business, Emmanuel! Furthermore, when I talk to you and look you in the eye, why don't you look me back in the eye?" My parents had taught me that anyone who won't look me in the eye probably could not be trusted.

Speaking to my friend as harshly as I did had embarrassed him. He was silent.

Finally, he said, "Ron, the reason we don't look you in the eye like you glare at us is because it's offensive, and we think you are going to start a fight with us. And the reason we ask these questions of where you've been, what you're doing, where you're going—it's our way of greeting people."

I felt so stupid! We had been in Cameroon for seven years, and only now was I learning the proper way to greet and be greeted by our national hosts!

Then I began thinking of the people I had offended with my "rudeness," the number of government officials I had called on, seated across from them behind their desk, trying to get eye contact and thus their attention. Later I learned those same eye contact and greeting issues are true across much of Africa.

Change is hard, but from then on, I made a conscious effort to look all over the place—behind, beside, above, but never into the eyes of the one to whom I was talking.

After returning to live in the United States, this cultural clue was appropriate and appreciated when engaging African personnel in Washington, DC, and New York City.

89

A SON BRINGS SALVATION

During a church worship service in a Wimbum community in west Cameroon, the worship leader read passages from an English Bible and verbally translated them line by line directly into Wimbum. As Pat Peck listened, she heard him read the familiar English passage, "He who has the son has life. He who does not have the son of God, has not life" (1 John 5:12). (King James Version)

However, the reader's interpretation of the text came out, "He who has a son has been saved, and he who doesn't have a son is not saved."

When asked what she thought of the translation, Pat replied, "Well, they probably knew the translation wasn't right, but also probably thought, 'Oh well, we can't understand the Bible, anyway.'"

Translating texts correctly into a language is extremely important. If translated passages are meaningless to the listeners, or even worse, give the wrong meaning, of what value are the efforts of a Bible translator?

90

YOU SPEAK OUR LANGUAGE LIKE A CHICKEN PECKS

In 1976 Karl and Winnie Grebe were in Canada on a needed home assignment session of R & R. The first years of living in the village had been extremely difficult for Winnie as the mother of two young boys, soon to be joined by a third.

In Canada she was speaking to a group of women in her church support group, telling them some anecdotes of village life back in Cameroon but also sharing from her heart.

The village ladies had told Winnie, "You talk our language like a chicken, pecking a little bit here and a little bit there." They were simply describing Winnie's limited Lamnso fluency.

However, she had taken it personally and was very distraught and discouraged. In fact, she broke down and cried. As she was telling this to her church support group, she also told them that she had decided not to return to Cameroon. The ladies gathered around her and prayed that God would remove her fear, that the Lamnso language would become easier for her, and that she would return with Karl to Cameroon.

She did return with Karl, and in the following months her Lamnso language fluency improved remarkably. Village women began attending literacy classes that Winnie taught and women's Bible studies that she led in the Lamnso language.

Was the women's support group in Canada, surrounding her with prayer, instrumental in the difference in her new attitude, perseverance, and commitment?

91

ROOF STOMPING

During our second four-year term of service in Cameroon, we rented a house in a neighborhood of Yaoundé, the capital city, near the airport. From our house it was an eleven-minute walk to the SIL center. The front porch side view was a valley frequently used by neighborhood kids to play sports.

One Saturday afternoon in 1978 while we were inside the house, loud stomping occurred, like that of an adult person jumping on top of the corrugated metal roofing of our house. I could hear the metal sheets crumpling under each stomp and wondered if the nails holding them would give way! Ruth heard it and our three children heard it. I ran outside, but could see no one on our roof, only a couple of birds. I asked our next-door neighbor sitting on his veranda with a clear view of our roof, and he said no one had been on it.

Then the stomping occurred a second time. When I asked our neighbor a second time if he was sure no one had been on our roof, he was adamant—no one had been on our roof!

I went back inside, remembering the strange, long parade of evenly spaced white lights in Papua New Guinea, and prayed, again asking God in the strong name of Jesus to protect us from evil. We did not hear any more roof stomping.

92

A DREAM SOLUTION

Over a period of four years, from 1978 through 1981, Ruth and I directed SIL's Africa Orientation Course in Cameroon. It was a three-month practical orientation to help SIL personnel newly arrived in Africa to learn to live simply, safely, and productively while acquiring an appreciation of African people and culture.

Participants included singles, married couples, and families with children. During the first month, in Yaoundé, the capital city, they learned a few basics, such as how to use public transport and shop and what the cultural expectations were. The second two months were spent living in a village, adjusting to life without the conveniences of potable running water, electricity, and appliances.

In 1978, the AOC orientees and I lived in the village of Bingela II in what was then the South-Central Province. The previous year's AOC director had also chosen Bingela II for their village phase. The session ended before they were able to complete a clean potable water project they had begun for the village.

The local people collected drinking water by dipping pots and pans in the same water puddle that livestock used and walked in as they drank. As a result, sickness was prevalent in the village.

The actual water source was pure, oozing out of the side of a small hill. But the water collected into a large puddle at the bottom of a hill into which animals urinated and defecated. Those of us at AOC also had to use that same water but knew to filter and boil it beforehand and encouraged our village hosts to do the same.

Isolating the clean water seemed doable, but collecting and storing it and finding a way to dispose of the perennial dirty water puddle were the challenges.

Before going to sleep one evening, I asked the Lord if he would please show me solutions. That night I dreamed about a practical solution. And the next morning I explained it to the orientees. Together we enlisted help of the local people in digging a dirt channel several feet deep that would drain the dirty puddle to a lower level where it ran off and dispersed. A fifty-five-gallon metal drum served as the form to build a cement reservoir of similar volume in which clean water collected and was kept isolated from the animals. To protect it from falling debris from trees and from critters such as goats and elephants, we built and secured a simple but strong roof over the reservoir.

Clean water could then be obtained only through a pipe installed a foot or so above where the puddle had been. One of the village men carved a piece of wood to plug up the pipe. Once the people learned to keep the pipe plugged after drawing water, clean water would accumulate in the cement reservoir and was available for others.

Livestock had to find water elsewhere but were not deprived. Mosquitoes were, however.

When the prefect (government district administrator) came by to check up on how we expatriates were living in a village, I showed him the improvements in the village water supply. He was somewhat amazed and asked where we had gotten the ideas for it. In my best French I told him about my prayer to the Lord, asking for solutions, which had then been given in a dream. He shook my hand, nodding his head in approval with a smile.

93

A HELPFUL PREFECT

By 1980 I had learned it was not only proper but also advantageous to seek the advice of the local government prefect in choosing a village for AOC's village training phase. The prefect asked for the criteria we wanted for such a village and promised to give me the names of two villages from which to choose.

A month later I visited both villages that he had suggested and informed him of the one I had selected. He was happy and asked that we stop at his residence on the day we moved to the village, which we did. Greeting all forty-two of us, he asked that we come inside his spacious home. A large, long table covered with an expansive array of refreshments and drinks awaited us.

After this delightful luncheon, we got back into the "bush taxis," and the prefect's aide led our caravan the rest of the way to the village. On orders of the prefect, all the roads had been graded the previous week. Upon entering the village all the vehicles drove under a tall, garlanded archway that the villagers had woven and erected in our honor.

Toward the end of training, we planned an overnight stay in the forest. The trainees and I spent that day in the forest fabricating beds out of inch-thick branches woven side by side with rope to sleep on. My son Charles, then ten years old, joined me. A small "bed" had been built for him by AOC trainees, and he quickly fell asleep.

I stretched out in another "bed" a few feet away from him and awoke during the night to the sound of a large jaw chewing noisily. But my flashlight revealed no large, four-legged critters—it revealed nothing, in fact. I just assumed it was a large pig satisfying its hunger pangs and drifted back to sleep. The critter did not awaken Charles.

The next day the village people were very upset that we had spent the night in the forest. They themselves would never do that because of taboos and traditional beliefs. Later I learned that before our arrival the prefect had delivered instructions to them that we were to be received and treated as special guests. His directive also included a threat that if anything bad happened to us while living with them, they would be severely punished. By our spending that night sleeping in the forest, we had complicated their ability to comply with the prefect's order to them.

Our campout had compromised their ability as hosts to protect us. They'd felt helpless. As AOC director I had not been made aware of the prefect's directive.

During that AOC session, the elders of a neighboring village extended an invitation to us to share a village-wide evening. We accepted and had a delightful dinner composed of a complete traditional meal with bottled beverages and fresh fruit for dessert. The people were delighted that we came. Each of our trainees gave the name of his home country and their destination in Africa. Most would be staying in Cameroon.

I thanked these hosts for their hospitality and for dinner, giving an explanation of how living in the village these few weeks helped prepare the young people for service in Cameroon or elsewhere in Africa. In return we gave small portions of chocolate and candy to our hosts and their children.

As the sun was about to set, we departed, walking the gravel road the mile back to the village where we were living. A military convoy of armored vehicles passed us going in the opposite direction. The last vehicle, a black Peugeot sedan, stopped. A rear window went down, and the deputy prefect greeted me, asking, "Is everything okay, Mr. Gluck?" I told him everything was fine and explained we had all been invited to dinner by another village and were just returning to our host village. He said, "Yes, I know," before waving good-bye and telling his driver to continue.

Then a question came to mind: what would result if a convoy of Cameroon's military vehicles had unexpectedly come upon our group of forty-plus white foreigners without their knowing of our presence in that region?

It was a scenario loaded with potential ramifications I didn't wish to contemplate, and I could only thank God that these AOC training sessions could be coordinated with government prefectures. Seeking and using their advice and welcoming their involvement amounted to an affirmation by the government of Cameroon of what we were doing. When the village people saw that our presence among them was coordinated by their own local authorities, their minds were put at ease, and they, too, affirmed what we were about. It had taken me two years—that is, two AOC sessions—to learn that collaborating with the government and avoiding surprises is important.

94

HEY! AREN'T YOU GOING TO STOP?

In the village I received word of two SIL visitors arriving from the United States, so I went to pick them up at the Yaoundé airport and drove them to the village where a session of AOC was in progress.

About three hundred feet before entering the village, we came upon the village chief walking on the road in the same direction. He was following behind a young woman and they were separated by maybe four to five feet.

I slowed down to greet the chief, but he was engaged in chiefly duties. In one hand he held a thin tree branch, using the leafy end as a switch on the backs of her legs. He was only switching her legs occasionally, but she shrieked with each blow. I'm sure they stung a little, though not as much as she would have wanted others to believe. As I drove slowly by them, not even turning my head to look, one of my backseat visitor passengers became irate.

"Hey! Aren't you going to stop?" he asked.

"No."

"Well, why not? Don't you see what he's doing?"

I explained to him that if he looked closely, the chief was not striking her hard; that, in fact, he was probably handling a disciplinary issue in their culture, and that we had no right to interfere. Besides, no one's life was being threatened.

Ray, his traveling companion, concurred. For years he had directed SIL's Jungle Training Camp in Mexico, helping orient new field personnel to live, study, and be productive in other cultures. Ruth and I had met Ray when we took SIL's Jungle Training in 1964.

95

LEVEL OR UNEVEN?

In the last month of the 1981 AOC session, I asked village leaders how we could tangibly express our appreciation to them for their hospitality. They said the people really needed a clinic. So we agreed to help them build one and were shown a site of undulating, uneven ground on which to build the structure. News of it traveled fast.

The next day, on instructions from the village school headmaster, each student came to the site with a pan or bowl from home. All morning long the children walked down a steep hill to the stream with the bowls and pans. They then returned, carrying the containers full of gravel and sand on their heads, and dumped the contents near the site. By noon there was a sizable pile of clean sand and gravel.

We placed an empty fifty-five-gallon drum next to the gravel pile, and by end of that day, the kids had filled it with water from the stream, using the same bowls and pans. With AOC funds, bags of cement and a concrete block mold were purchased. On the ground we mixed cement and gravel with water and then placed it inside a wooden form outlining the floor. (The

AOC guys had staked out a rectangular site of roughly fifteen by twenty feet.)

Simple technology was used to help pour a level cement floor. A stick approximately seven inches long was placed in a big kitchen bowl of water. Sighting down the stick to each of the four corners of the site was a simple way to determine where to add or take away dirt in order to end up with a level floor— well, somewhat level.

The deputy prefect happened by at that moment and watched me sighting down the floating stick and instructing guys on each corner how much dirt to add or remove. He was perturbed and asked what I was doing. I tried to explain the sighting and floor leveling procedure to him but could see he was not a happy camper.

"We don't do it that way," he said abruptly. "We don't disturb the dirt. We just pour the cement onto the ground. We don't move dirt." His last statement provided a possible clue. *By disturbing the dirt were we invading a spirit world?* I wondered. A level floor was not deemed important.

And so a decision was needed—whether to build their way or build our way, whether to pour an uneven cement floor or a level cement floor.

Would this be their clinic or the white man's clinic? We, of course, wanted it to be theirs, and therefore poured an undulating cement floor, conforming to the uneven ground. The villagers were happy.

It was a heartburn moment for me. In Western culture, purposefully laying an unlevel cement floor seems tantamount to a deceit in construction, but then again, a level floor is simply a cultural issue, not a moral value.

The AOC participants shook their heads in dismay. This was a cross-cultural lesson I will never, ever forget.

96

ABOUT 1935 . . .

Solomon Nforgwei obtained his doctorate in education at the University of Michigan. He was also my first Cameroonian paying airplane passenger in 1973. Before his return to Cameroon, a fellow university student had invited Sol to go along to the campus store, and Sol accepted the invite. While at the store, in the checkout line, his friend suddenly turned to him and asked, "Sol, how old are you?"

Sol told me, "I was embarrassed to be asked that question, so did not answer."

His friend then repeated the question, only much louder. "Sol, how old are you?!" All the other students in line also turned, waiting to hear Sol's answer.

Finally Sol replied. "I don't know how old I am. When I was born, my birth was never recorded because my language has never been written." Other students in line hearing his answer laughed and laughed. And he himself laughed as he told me the story. So I said to him, "Well, you travel a lot and carry a Cameroonian passport. What birth date is in it?"

He opened it up and showed it to me. Adjacent to birth date was handwritten, "About 1935."

Sol remained a close friend until his death in 2002. I never realized how much his life influenced me.

97

FAITH AND HEARTBURN:
A CLASH OF VALUES

Solomon's personal integrity and faith caused "heartburn" for some. After arriving back in Cameroon with a doctorate in education, Sol accepted a teaching position in a government secondary school. However, soon thereafter, the president of Cameroon named Solomon vice minister of agriculture.

One of Sol's responsibilities as the vice minister was oversight of Cameroon's contracts with foreign timber companies, as the southern third of the country is heavily forested. It was a lucrative business for the government and for foreign companies receiving contracts to cut and export Cameroon's previously unharvested timber.

Strange things began happening after he assumed his official duties. His responsibility as vice minister required frequent travel outside of Cameroon, and on such trips it would not be unusual for him to find upon entering his hotel room an envelope containing large amounts of currency with more promised if Solomon would grant timber rights to certain companies.

When the next president took office, he not only retained Sol as vice minister of agriculture, but also named him chairman of the National Commission on Human Rights and Freedoms. Sol's workload therefore increased, resulting in an increasing clash of values with others.

That commission was given a budget. But when Sol refused to play the money game that others played, he then learned that others, unnamed in government, also had access to that budget and began withdrawing funds from the commission account.

Furthermore, on returning home from human rights conferences outside the country, he found that his baggage was being tampered with and papers stolen. Also, personal notes he had taken at the conferences were missing. Someone in government confronted him about his reports on the issues of human rights and corruption in Cameroon, saying that because of Solomon's reports, Cameroon was no longer receiving development funding from international agencies. In fact, increasing amounts of money began to disappear from the human rights account, curtailing all his foreign travel. On our last visit to Cameroon, in 1996, Sol's wife, Elizabeth, told Ruth that she was concerned because of death threats being made against her husband.

Sol told me that the president of Cameroon several times had requested of him, "Come see me. I want to talk with you." Solomon told me each time he had tried to make an appointment to see the president, a secretary either refused or found a reason not to schedule one.

During that 1996 visit, I called on Sol in his office. He asked his aides to leave the room and then confirmed to me the death threats he was receiving. Together we got on our knees. With my arm around him I prayed for our almighty God's protection.

Question: did Sol have a greater impact in the vice minister of agriculture and human rights chairman positions than he would have had by pasturing a church?

98

FRIDAY NIGHT PRAYER BREAKFASTS

In the 1990s the president of Cameroon received an invitation from the US Congress to attend the annual National Prayer Breakfast in Washington, DC, but asked Solomon to go in his place. Solomon went and was so taken by the concept of praying for parliamentarians and leaders in government that on his return to Cameroon he began visiting other government ministers just to pray with them. They in turn asked Solomon to pray with their staffs and also took him to their homes to pray with members of their families. Before long a small group of close friends accompanied Solomon on his prayer missions with other cabinet ministers. In addition, this growing group began meeting Friday evenings after work to pray for leaders in their government and their nation.

Inwardly I laughed when hearing of the "Friday night prayer breakfasts." But then, on reflection, it actually made sense. They were breaking an all-day fast on Fridays by eating dinner together—*after* praying for the leaders of their nation.

Whenever I visited Sol in his office, there were always people outside the door waiting to see the "pastor," wanting his help with personal problems. They came to his office or his home at all hours, knowing he was a man of God who would listen and pray with them.

During one of Sol's business trips to Washington, my wife, Ruth, was in the hospital, and he suggested we go and pray with her. When he had finished praying for her, he said to me, "Let's go around and pray with other patients in the hospital." He introduced himself as a pastor from Africa and prayed for at least a dozen patients on that floor whom neither he nor I had ever met. Not one of the patients refused his offer to pray.

When was the last time any of us went to pray with and for someone we know, let alone someone we don't?

99

I'LL SEE YOU IN HEAVEN

Three of Solomon Nforgwei's children received their higher education at Morgan State University outside of Baltimore, Maryland. Sol usually stayed with them whenever he came to the States.

On his last visit to the United States, he sought medical treatment for his sickle cell anemia liver condition. Medical doctors informed him that without a liver transplant he would soon die. In relating this to me over the phone, he added, "I just don't have the money, so I won't be around too much longer. I'll see you in heaven." And in June 2002, his earthly life ended.

Also in 2002, a translation of the New Testament was completed in Wimbum, Sol's mother tongue.

Were these two events coincidental in that a permanent Wimbum witness of God, the Limbum New Testament, replaced Sol, God's mortal Wimbum witness?

AGARUNA OF PERU

In 1963, when Ruth and I attended an SIL orientation at the University of Oklahoma in Norman, we were intrigued listening to Millie Larson of SIL's Peru branch explaining how she overcame a translation problem. Unable to identify a term or phrase in the Agaruna language that conveyed an equivalent of love as used in John 3:16, she made up a "for instance" to find one. Millie posed this question to her language helper: "How would you react if someone stole something you highly value, such as your fish hooks?"

The language helper responded, "I would have such strong feelings (*senchi*) for that person that I would . . ." and he then described punishment he would inflict on the thief.

Senchi means *strongly*. You can strongly get angry or you can strongly dislike or whatever. The translation has *senchi aneau*. *Aneau* means the emotion of caring. *Senchi aneau* conveys extreme caring action.

That is the phrase that Millie used in John 3:16—feelings requiring extreme action. "God had such strong feelings for the world that he gave His only Son . . ."

TZELTAL OF MEXICO

In 1964, Jungle Camp was required training for new Wycliffe recruits. Our session took place among rural communities of Tzeltal people in southern Mexico. Ruth and I learned that in the Tzeltal tongue, the verb for *believe* and the verb for *obey* are the same. Therefore, if you believe something, you act in obedience to it.

Had God prepared the Tzeltal people for his Word long before their exposure to it?

GOLIN OF PNG

Gordon Bunn, an Australian in PNG, and his wife, Ruth, lived in a village near the Omkalai airstrip where they were trying to unravel and reassemble the Golin language. Gordon attempted translating Psalm 24:3–4: "Who may ascend the mountain of the LORD? Who may stand in his holy place? The one who has clean hands and a pure heart, who does not trust in an idol or swear by a false god." (King James Version)

The "clean hands" reference was problematic. Gordon found it made no sense to his language helper. Anyone with clean hands could not have a pure heart, climb the mountain of the Lord, nor stand in his holy place.

Why? Someone having clean hands meant that person was lazy, did not work, and therefore could not have a pure heart.

How would you, reader, translate it?

What is the meaning of having clean hands and a pure heart? Would "dirty hands" be a possible translation? Or might it refer to one's deeds and thoughts, external actions and internal motivations, such as those who have not worshipped idols, as SIL's translation consultant Dr. Ellis Deibler suggests?

SHEEP ARE UNKNOWN;
PIGS ARE POPULAR

In New Guinea, some folk have heard of sheep, but sheep are not commonly known. In Pidgin English, sheep are called *sipsip*. In most areas of PNG, pigs are the dominant domestic animal.

Therefore, the numerous references and stories of sheep in the Scriptures are meaningless to many New Guineans. But they love their pigs. In the 1960s it was not uncommon to see a woman nursing a child on one breast and a small piglet on the other.

When the Scriptures reference Jesus as the "Lamb of God," it frequently is translated as the young of God's *sipsip*, or pig. Westerners might find this offensive, but it makes all the difference in the world to the people of Papua New Guinea.

104

JESUS LOST HIS NAME FOR US

SIL's Marilyn Laszlo in Papua New Guinea searched long for a term in the Sepik Iwam language meaning *death*. Then she heard of two Sepik Iwam men who had gotten lost in a forest and were fearful of losing their names—or dying.

Learning that phrase enabled Marilyn to translate "Jesus died on the cross for us" as "Jesus lost his name for us."

UPSTAIRS?

Acts 9:36–37 tells briefly of Dorcas, a good woman who became sick and died. Her body was washed and placed upstairs, where it was prepared for burial, according to custom.

The Lamso people of Cameroon in the 1970s did not have two-story houses. A literal translation would have meant that the body of Dorcas was put in the ceiling, a common cultural practice, where smoke from cooking fires would rise and preserve the body for years by keeping bugs out.

So Karl and Winnie Grebe, wanting to avoid this connotation, modified a translation of the verse to "Her body was washed and placed in another room where it was prepared for burial."

A REALLY GOOD FRIEND

Among the Cakchiquel people of Guatemala, it's one thing to have a friend, but, as William Cameron Townsend learned, a really good friend will pick the lice out of your hair.

107

A GUATEMALAN'S LIFE PERSPECTIVE

Wayne Huff of the SIL Guatemala branch told me that two weeks after American astronaut Neil Armstrong's 1969 walk on the moon, Wayne told his language helper, Chico, that news and asked him if he wouldn't also like to walk on the moon.

Chico paused a very long time, reflecting on the question, then, answered: "No, that isn't what I want to do. Friend, what I want to do is learn to read. Then I can read what the Creator of the moon says and teach others about walking down here on earth."

Who placed that burning desire of knowing how to read and teach in Chico's heart?

GLANCING BACKWARD

Everyone has close calls, moments of danger when the immediate outcome is in question. If disaster is averted, we usually exhale a quick *whew*, dismissing factors over which we may have had no control. However, frightening scenarios of what might have been linger and dissipate more slowly. Eventually they, too, are dismissed, and we move on.

Some events in this book occurred nearly fifty years ago, many details of which this former bush pilot remembers vividly. Not all of them were flight related. When they occurred, lessons were learned, sometimes more than once, because on occasion I was "too busy" to take the time needed time to think through why they really happened.

Since retiring in 2007, I have been in active backward-glance mode, and being forcefully reminded that over the years another person, the Creator who superintends factors over which we have no control, was and remains active in my life and in the lives of many, many others.

If a story of my mine resurrects scary memories of impending disaster averted in your own life, review that period of living. You may uncover new appreciation of his care in your own journey. To encourage, not to entertain, is the primary purpose of publishing these stories.

109

RETIREMENT PROVOKED
A TRANSITION

In 1959 all sixty or so of us employees in the J&L Steel big engineering office in Pittsburgh, Pennsylvania, were summoned to the front and listened as the chief engineer praised an older employee for years of faithful service. He was then given a gold wristwatch, a $200 US government savings bond, and a certificate of service. That was it. Retirement for him officially began.

We all applauded and went back to our desks, but my mind was reeling from a swirling tornado strike of new questions. Was what I had just witnessed the same work climax I wanted in fifty years? What was my goal in life? I had not given much thought to having a life goal or plan, let alone work on one. At age twenty-six I determined not to wait fifty years to find answers and identify plan A. God had created me, so he would know—but how would I find his affirmation to answers?

There is a clue in the second chapter of Proverbs regarding the search for wisdom. If one searched for it like hidden treasure, leaving no stone unturned, then insight and understanding would be granted. It had just become apparent that knowing how I should use the remainder of my life would be worth more than gold. I promised God I would spend all the money I had saved, $1,000 at the time, to learn what path he wanted me to follow.

In 1960 I transferred to the J&L plant in Cleveland, Ohio, driving home to Pittsburgh on weekends for air guard duty. In Cleveland I met people my age preparing for overseas mission service, and even though I began supporting them financially, I did not believe that kind of service was for me. On a weekend in Keswick, Canada, I met Karl Warnholtz, a potato farmer who forcefully suggested I use my flying skills to serve the Lord. It was plain that he meant traditional missionary service, but I believed crop dusters, airline pilots, and air force and air national guard pilots also serve the Lord!

Over breakfast, Ernie, a used car dealer in Cleveland, gave me the name of JAARS, which at the time stood for Jungle Aviation and Radio Service. He said they use pilots to fly Bible translators into remote areas of the world.

My postcard question to JAARS was "Does your outfit use ex-military pilots?" The return letter by Merrill Piper said it depended on passing a flight and mechanical evaluation, a practical Bible test, and interviews. Also, I would need aircraft mechanic ratings before applying, because JAARS pilots maintained the planes they flew. I loved working with my hands. Gradually the thrill of air guard flying diminished. But I did not want to make a decision based on feelings. How could I know if JAARS really would be plan A? Flying was a skill in which I was trained, but was JAARS in his plan for me? Had pursuit of an electrical engineering degree simply been a waste?

A story is recorded in the sixth chapter of Judges in the Old Testament when God chose Gideon, a warrior, to lead the Israelites into battle. Gideon was hesitant, not really sure God would lead him to victory. Being unsure, he made a decision by using a piece of fleece, dependent on an intervention of the morning dew by God, on two occasions.

Then Gideon said to God, "If you are truly going to use me to rescue Israel as you promised, prove it to me in this way. I will put a wool fleece on the threshing floor tonight. If the fleece is wet with dew in the morning but the ground is dry, then I will know that you are going to help me rescue Israel as you promised." And that is just what happened. When Gideon got up early the next morning, he squeezed the fleece and wrung out a whole bowlful of water.

Then Gideon said to God, "Please don't be angry with me, but let me make one more request. Let me use the fleece for one more test. This time let the fleece remain dry while the ground around it is wet with dew." So that night God did as Gideon asked. The fleece was dry in the morning, but the ground was covered with dew. (New Living Translation)

Then Gideon decided God was indeed trustworthy, followed his instructions, and led the Israelites to victory.

In my quest I sought guidance with a fleece of my own design over five days of flying. Not much can happen in a Piper Cub, but on the final day, a severe war of airsickness suddenly erupted in my stomach. I was at five-thousand-feet altitude over a small Ohio town, Twinsburg. The air was cool and calm, but my whole body was perspiring profusely. About to empty my tummy and lose everything, I pulled out a plastic bag and held it over my mouth while yelling to God, "Lord, you know if I vomit I'm not gonna go!"—meaning that if I vomited, I would not pursue flying with JAARS or any other mission any further. After I landed back at Cuyahoga County Airport, his response to my fleece slowly sunk in. The perspiration and airsickness over Twinsburg had quietly subsided. I had not vomited. I had not even belched a loud burp!

Based on that experience, the next step seemed clear. In May 1962, I enrolled at the Spartan School of Aeronautics in order to obtain the aircraft mechanic training that JAARS required of their pilots and quit my engineering job with J&L Steel Corp.

During that first month in Tulsa, Oklahoma, I began corresponding with Ruth Ann Bishop, a nurse I had met in Cleveland. In fact, she had taken me to dinner to say good-bye the evening before I left for Spartan. Based on my previous dating experiences, I decided another fleece was in order before considering a further relationship with her.

We married three months later, honeymooning in Tulsa during the nine additional months I attended Spartan. Finding a new supervisory nursing position there enabled Ruth to put food on the table for us both. Karl Gruber, a former airline pilot already with JAARS and also enrolled at Spartan helped me obtain a flight instructor rating. Giving flight instruction enabled me to accrue flying hours in light aircraft and pay the sixty-dollar monthly house rent.

The following summer, we attended the Summer Institute of Linguistics. I was given a JAARS flight evaluation, and Wycliffe Bible Translators accepted us as candidates. After more orientation, we accepted an assignment as pilot-mechanic to what was then the Territory of Papua and New Guinea, arriving in March 1965 with our first child of six months, Cheryl.

Karl, the Canadian potato farmer, and Ernie, the used car dealer, had each been in my life briefly.

Questions

Did I meet them solely for the purpose of being steered to JAARS?

Was God using my personal quest for guidance as a way to teach them too?

Ernie sold me a car and did well after acquiring a new car dealership. After our acceptance by Wycliffe and JAARS, Karl continued farming potatoes and supported us in prayer and finances for more than forty years.

110

BOTTOM LINE: HEY! BE THANKFUL

Some will describe the preceding pages as luck or navel gazing or simply say that stuff happens. For me, another conclusion seems obvious.

1. Yes, stuff happens—because, "God causes everything to work together" (Romans 8:28 New Living Translation).
2. The truth of Romans 8:28 correlates to another verse— "He is not far from any one of us. For in Him we live and move and have our being" (Acts 17:27–28 New Living Translation)—reinforcing each person's distinct unique existence.

   Being means existing, living in the present—an ongoing, continuing process. And our "being," or life on earth, will end when it falls within that Romans 8:28 parameter of God "causing everything to work together."

So, my bottom line is this.

Hey! Be thankful . . . each day . . . the present is a gift from the Giver of life. Tomorrow isn't a given

TECHNICAL STUFF

Aircraft Used:

- Cessna 185, six-place, tail-wheel, high-wing, single-engine 285-horsepower with belly cargo pod; used in PNG
- Cessna U206, six-place, high-wing, single-engine, 285-horsepower, turbocharged with tricycle landing gear, belly cargo pod; used in PNG because of mountainous terrain
- Cessna U206, same as above but 300-horsepower and non-turbocharged; used in Cameroon
- Piper PA23-250, Aztec D model, twin-engine (both turbocharged), 250-horsepower, low-wing and seven-place modified seating; used in PNG
- Hughes 300 helicopter, three-place; used in PNG

Note

Turbocharger – equipment installed on internal combustion engines that enables maximum sea level engine power performance at much higher altitudes.

--P-factor is asymmetric propeller loading. The descending right side of the prop blade (as seen from the rear) has a higher angle of attack than the upward-moving blade on the left side and thus provides more thrust. It causes the plane to yaw to the left. On single-engine aircraft with a tail wheel, for example, ground loops can result on takeoff if insufficient opposite rudder is applied to counteract P-factor. It is most noticeable on takeoff with a nose-high attitude or high angle of attack. Aircraft with tricycle landing gear maintain a level attitude on the takeoff roll run and thus experience little P-factor effect during takeoff.

--Weight and balance factors limit the loading of airplanes. In general, seating heavier people or placing heavier cargo over or under the wings or toward the front will usually assure the center of gravity of an airplane within the effective range of the flight controls.

ACKNOWLEDGMENTS

The stories compiled herein would not have occurred without the faithful financial support of prayer partners. Ruth and I will never be able to thank them adequately. Their life values parallel our own, and we are deeply grateful to them.

These slices of life involve faith and flying, culture, language morsels, and translation gems and cover three periods.

-Papua New Guinea: 1965–1970
-Cameroon: 1970–1981
-Washington, DC, and New York City: 1981–2007

"Language, Culture, Faith, Translation, and Life Morsels" is the fourth segment, containing gems that encourage us today.

In 2007, I was stumped, wondering how to fit a report summarizing our forty-four years of service into a forty-minute time slot. Over the next two weeks, after seeking the Creator's help in memory recall, my recollection was overflowing, filled with many events, including precise details, that had occurred a half century ago. Since giving that report six years ago, a flow of events continues accruing in my memory. A few accounts involving errors in judgment, questionable choices, and lessons learned are included in the text.

BEFORE SIGNING OFF

Each fall delicious McIntosh and Northern Spy apples filled branches of three tall trees next to the chicken house in the rear of my parent's Castle Shannon, PA property. And each fall kids from the adjoining school playground threw stones up into the tree in hopes of knocking down fresh apples. My parents didn't mind sharing the apples, but many of the stones fell onto the chicken house putting holes in the tarpaper roof. Dad assigned me the task of roof repair after apple seasons.

Mother heard me grumbling about it and said, "I'll fix 'em." The next day she handed me a notebook sized piece of cardboard on which she had printed in red, THOU GOD SEEST ME with the Genesis 13:16 King James reference. She weather proofed it in plastic wrap instructing me to post it on the nearest tree to and facing the playground. I tried telling her it would do no good, but she was insistent, so I did as told and promptly forgot about it.

Two weeks later, she and Dad realized the stone throwing had stopped. In fact the last roof repair lasted for close to three years. By then wind had carried away Mom's weathered sign. In hindsight, this teenager glimpsed the power of God's Word to change human behavior without the intervention of another person.

In 1961 fourteen years later, I learned this principle is the same reason that SIL, JAARS and WBT exist. People without access to God's Word in a language they understand are enabled to discover – by hearing or reading it for themselves in a language they think in, their mother tongue – principles for living that our Creator has given. I wanted to be part of this undertaking.

That reason is also why new national Bible translation agencies such as BTA (Bible Translation Association) in PNG and CABTAL (Cameroon Association for Bible Translation and Literacy) have started, joining a growing global alliance of national translation agencies – hastening fulfillment of the last commission (see end of Matthew 28th chapter) that Jesus left his followers.

SIL International
Website: www.sil.org
Phone: 972-708-7400

JAARS
Website: www.jaars.org
Phone: 800-890-0628

Wycliffe Bible Translators
Website: www.wycliffe.org
Phone: 800-992-5433

Wycliffe Global Alliance
Website: http://www.wycliffe.net/

ABOUT THE AUTHOR

At 81 years of age I have learned a little.

An Electrical Engineering BS degree from Carnegie Tech, flight skills and discipline acquired from U.S. Air Force Aviation Cadet training, flying with the Pennsylvania Air National Guard 147th Fighter Interceptor Squadron and aviation mechanical training from Spartan School of Aeronautics helped meet stringent requirements of JAARS, the technical arm of Wycliffe Bible Translators. Serving 44 years under partner agencies--Wycliffe, JAARS and SIL International, abroad and in the U.S.A.--included teachable moments. While documenting these events recently, incidents surfaced that I had not previously questioned; third party involvement, sequencing, weather and other incidents beyond my control that had converged--central to what happened. Can they merely be viewed as "co-incidents" and dismissed?

In that I flew over 5,000 hours in some of the most remote, uncharted areas of the world without mishap can only be attributed to the prayers of God's people, His grace and excellent maintenance by fellow JAARS technicians. Questions posed after story segments may help to reflect on how the Creator remains in the business of impacting personal lives.

Since 1981, my wife and I have lived in Arlington, Virginia near our nation's capital. This has enabled us to have a small part in promoting effective cooperation and goodwill between SIL, foreign governments and international organizations.

CPSIA information can be obtained at www.ICGtesting.com
Printed in the USA
LVOW11s0036041114

411844LV00001B/1/P